# *Natural Wonders of*
# ᵀᴴᴱ FLORIDA KEYS

## *Exploring Wild and Scenic Places*

DEBORAH STRAW

## COUNTRY ROADS PRESS
*NTC/Contemporary Publishing Group*

**Library of Congress Cataloging-in-Publication Data**

Straw, Deborah.
   Natural wonders of the Florida Keys : exploring wild and scenic places /
Deborah Straw.
      p.   cm. — (Natural wonders)
   Includes bibliographical references (p. 135) and index.
   ISBN 1-56626-047-7
     1. Florida Keys (Fla.) Guidebooks.   2. Natural areas—Florida—
Florida Keys Guidebooks.   3. Parks—Florida—Florida Keys Guidebooks.
I. Title.  II. Series.
F317.M7 S53   1999
917.59′410463—dc21                   99-29933
                                            CIP

Cover and interior design by Nick Panos
Cover photograph: Bahia Honda State Park. Copyright © Jeff Greenberg/
Panoramic Images, Chicago, 1999
Interior illustrations and map copyright © Gigi Bayliss. Spot illustrations copyright
© Barbara Kelley
Picture research by Elizabeth Broadrup Lieberman
Typesetting by VARDA Graphics, Inc.

Published by Country Roads Press
A division of NTC/Contemporary Publishing Group, Inc.
4255 West Touhy Avenue, Lincolnwood (Chicago), Illinois 60646-1975 U.S.A.
Copyright © 1999 by Deborah Straw
Printed in the United States of America
International Standard Book Number: 1-56626-047-7

99 00 01 02 03 04 ML 19 18 17 16 15 14 13 12 11 10 9 8 7 6 5 4 3 2 1

*Dedicated to Donald Straw, 1908–1998*

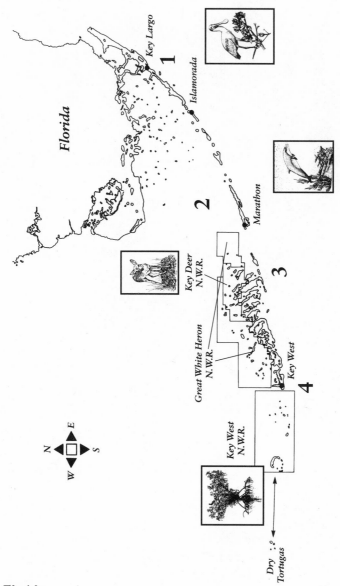

Florida
*(Figures correspond with chapter numbers.)*

# Contents

## 5 Nature Organizations 121

# Acknowledgments

First I want to thank my parents, Phyllis and Donald Straw, who instilled in me a great love of nature and of the printed word. My husband, Bruce Conklin, has always supported my writing and research, and provided lots of computer and editing assistance. My women writers group, in existence for 10 years, has helped enormously with editing and encouragement: thanks to Michelle Demers, Susan Green, and Maggie Maurice. Patti Lanich provided much needed technical assistance; Linda Bland gave professional advice. Thank you to all the Keys people who provided support, encouragement, and invaluable information: Becky Barron, Rick Sawicki, Barry Stieglitz, Tom Hambright, and Lynda Schuh, in particular. And to our good friend, George Fontana, without whom this project could never have happened.

I also want to thank my first publisher, John White, and my first editor, Liza Fosburgh, for accepting my proposal and for believing in the project from the beginning, and thanks to Ray Jones, my final editor, for seeing this book through to completion. My fondest hope is that this book will play a small part in saving the Keys' natural beauty for many more generations.

Note: As the Florida Keys tend to be a somewhat transient place, I have not listed times or prices for many sites. These change somewhat seasonally, and commercial enterprises sometimes close suddenly. It's always wise to check by phone before visiting any site.

I have included all sites and commercial enterprises possible. Some people did not return my calls nor answer my inquiries, so they are not included. Also, I have not included all available dolphin activities or so-called "eco-trips" because some treat creatures and their habitats in an environmental manner I do not wish to promote. Because of Hurricane Georges' impact in the fall of 1998, some outdoor facilities and events may have changed slightly. The beaches and trees, in particular, suffered great damage. Finally, I did visit or participate in 90 percent of the sites and activities listed herein; based on careful research, I believe the remaining 10 percent are really doing what they say they are. If anyone finds anything unethical or untrue in any of the listings, please contact me through my publisher to ensure a correction in future editions.

# Introduction

Not all nature lovers are enamored of strenuous physical challenges. Not all of us like to bike 20 miles a day, or sleep in the snow or near a marshy mangrove forest with insects attempting to carry the tent away. Not all of us are comfortable swimming or navigating boats, and we don't all carry field guides and backpacks. We don't all have degrees in botany or natural science. Nature lovers come in all sizes and degrees of physical fitness, and many of us just love to study all things natural, without taking great risks. Some of us find adventure in just looking at nature's brilliant colors and forms.

This is the audience for whom I have written this book—people like me. I once wrote a poem about how wildlife inspires me during my travels, even in the urban settings of Paris and Washington, D.C. I may not remember the name of the Picasso painting or the sculpture by Rodin, but I'll never forget seeing pink flamingos at the Jardin des Plantes in the City of Light, or the pair of peacocks next to the James McNeill Whistler Peacock Room at the Freer Gallery in our nation's capital.

What could be better than making eye contact with a huge, gentle manatee near the Turtle Kraals in Key West? Or seeing your first Key deer, of which only 300 still exist, on a tiny group of islands centered in Big Pine Key? Nothing. At least not for me, though I also adore cities, museums, culinary adventures, and books.

Animals, birds, and flowers have enriched my life; they perk up my lagging spirits and serve as my muses. Did I mention my first glimpse of black squirrels in Ottawa or the trapped pigeon in a storefront on 42nd Street in New York? Unforgettable. I seldom go hiking, especially up great mountains. I generally avoid places where there are swarms of mosquitoes, rattlesnakes underfoot, or black bears nearby. But I love to walk and see what I can see on fairly flat terrain. I can do more than 10 miles a day, taking periodic rests. I visit parks, wildlife rehabilitation centers, beaches, aquariums, and dolphin sanctuaries. I've seen lots of birds, bugs, and flowers, often in unexpected places.

I also love to read about nature, to watch nature movies, to look at people's slides about various species. I've attended lectures on topics from hurricanes to hibiscus. And I like to buy nature-related objects, particularly if the maker is a local craftsperson or if some of the proceeds go to a charitable nature organization.

Just as I'll never forget my first experience with the manatee or the lovely, fragile Key deer, I will remember the Dolphin Research Center's great work and the animals' grace as they leapt out of the water, and my first sighting of the shy burrowing owl on the beach in Marathon. I loved the Greenpeace shop on Duval Street and mourn its closing. None of these moments were risky or dangerous.

So, I have chosen to introduce you, my kind of nature lover, to the Keys. In these pages are what I consider the best places to see wildlife, the best books and periodicals to read, and the most worthwhile organizations for volunteer work or donations. I've even included some organizations that help domestic animals, in particular, cats. Hundreds of emaciated strays need attention and food in the lower Keys. Some of this information is available in the local papers and tourist brochures, but much of it I have gathered on my extended visits to the Keys. Some is known only by the locals (and now you).

To see exotic, colorful species, you won't have to hike miles, swim in 20-foot-deep pools, or camp in the blistering sun—unless you want to. You won't have to climb mountains; the Keys are blessedly flat. But you will have to walk, be curious, and be willing to be surprised and charmed.

# History and Geography

The first Europeans to look upon the shores of Florida were the Spanish, led by Juan Ponce de Leon, then governor of Puerto Rico, in 1513. Seeking riches and natives to capture as slaves, he gave the area its name, "La Florida" (the Flowery Land), and claimed it for Spain. Until they were killed by Europeans or fled to West Indian islands, native tribes inhabited southeastern Florida. Spain and Britain alternated ownership of the Florida peninsula until 1821 when Florida was ceded to the United States.

The Keys' first residents were the Matecumbe Indians, a tribe descended from Eurasians. They lived peacefully with 500 species of birds and 7,800 lakes, and they worshiped the sun. Not many Americans lived in South Florida until the late 1800s because much of it was marsh and swamp. Most people traveled by boat because few highways existed. This was the frontier.

Key West, or Cayo Hueso (Bone Key), is the United States' southernmost city. It is named for the bones Ponce de Leon found here, the result of wars by rival groups of Indians who, because of religious custom or the hard limestone ground, did not bury their dead.

In the late 1700s, the lower Keys were home to rich shipping merchants and infamous pirates like Blackbeard and Captain Kidd. In 1822, Key West was sold to John Simonton;

the island was declared a port of entry and its first customs house opened.

Other historical highlights include the year 1831, when the first handmade-cigar factory was established by William H. Wall in Key West. After the Civil War, cigar manufacturing became one of the principal economic forces in Key West, and the city became the 13th largest port in the country. It was an international port of call for ships engaged in Atlantic, Caribbean, and Gulf trade, and the fishing and salvage industries flourished. In 1880, Key West also became the largest city in Florida (population 9,890).

One of the most influential people in southern Florida's history was Henry Flagler. He wanted to extend the Florida East Coast Railroad from Miami (by then a boomtown) to Key West, where a ferry would then deliver passengers 90 more miles to Havana. In 1896, the railroad only reached Miami. The railroad, completed in Key West in 1912, was hailed by speakers at its dedication as "the Eighth Wonder of the World." Unfortunately, on Labor Day 1935, a hurricane destroyed Flagler's prize railroad.

Next, engineers wanted to connect the Keys with causeways, with no more than six miles of bridges. But the locals disagreed, claiming it would prevent the flow of seawater between the islands during storms and would cause flooding. The Overseas Highway (Route 1) was completed in 1928 and is punctuated by 42 bridges. The Seven-Mile Bridge just south of Marathon, also destroyed in the 1935 hurricane and rebuilt in 1982, is the longest of its kind in the world.

In the early part of the century, a ride on the Overseas Highway from Miami to Key West took up to eight hours, four of which were spent on a ferry between Lower Matecumbe Key and No Name Key. That entire trip now takes around four hours.

During the early and mid-20th century, Key West became popular as a destination and as a home base for famous people. In 1927, the Key West airport was constructed, which encouraged more tourism. Today, 70 percent of the island's economy is linked to tourism. Writers such as Tennessee Williams, Ernest Hemingway, and Elizabeth Bishop found the island city a great place to live and write. President Harry Truman established the Little White House, now a museum, here in 1946. The U.S. Navy established a base here in 1939 and continues to be a constant presence.

Geographically, the Keys are exceedingly flat and have large amounts of surface water, i.e., lakes, canals, rivers, and ponds. The Keys are actually a chain of dozens of tiny islands shaping an archipelago stretching approximately 125 miles from Key Largo to Key West. Florida does have other keys (coral islets) farther north, but they are not part of the southernmost chain called the Florida Keys. Seen from the air, the Keys look like a shimmering necklace in an azure sea. The Keys are, on average, 2 to 4 feet above sea level, with the highest islands at 18 feet. The highest points are the landfills, particularly one on Stock Island, just north of Key West.

The 5,000-year-old islands are made of hard limestone, the remains of an old coral reef, the Key Largo Limestone. The lush vegetation is West Indian. Trade winds (and occasionally hurricanes) from the southeast bring seeds and even some small animals from the West Indies. The most obvious trees are the palms, which exist in at least 10 native species and dozens of other exotic species. Animal and bird life is abundant and colorful. Several habitats exist: the only coral reefs in the continental United States; four species of mangroves—water-loving trees with large roots that thrive in tidal zones; pinelands—pine forest on limestone—found primarily in the Everglades and on Big Pine Key; sandy and rock, or crushed-shell, beaches; and hammocks—isolated stands of hardwood trees and associated plants.

# Weather and Clothes

South Florida is hot and quite humid; the sun shines almost every day. The intensity of those rays can take you by surprise, especially if you're used to a rather gray climate like mine in northern New England. But, surprisingly, the Keys don't feel as hot as many parts of the South because of the frequent breezes from the ocean. In fact, residents of northern Florida often vacation in the Keys during the summer. It often rains in summer and fall, and sometimes there are storms with high winds. This cools things down considerably, at least for an hour or so.

During the winter months, December through February, the temperatures are generally in the 60s and 70s. It has never even frosted here, as it does farther north. In Homestead (approximately 35 miles south of Miami), it once dropped to 27 degrees, but this is rare, indeed. There are extremes, of course. This past winter, the thermometer plummeted to 48 degrees in Key West in early February, setting a record in a town where almost no one owns a heater. Within two or three days the temperature was back up to around 80.

The rest of the year, March through November, it's considerably hotter, generally hovering between 80 and 95. The air is more humid; there are more mosquitoes. August is generally the warmest month. During the summer months, people move slower. Many natives take a siesta just like the Italians. The best times to walk or hike are early morning, before 10:00 A.M., and evening, as it stays light quite late here.

From late August to mid-October is peak hurricane season; it's when Hurricane Andrew struck with such force. Fortunately, however, Andrew passed just north of the Keys. A hurricane hasn't hit as far south as Key West since 1935. People who live here, of course, are prepared, hanging hurricane shutters on their homes, storing lots of edible provisions and candles during the fall months, and plotting how they will safely navigate congested Route 1 if the need arises. Before heading to the Keys during peak hurricane season, it is wise to check the National Weather Service for weather activity in the area.

One advantage of this season is that the roads, parks, and restaurants aren't as full of tourists as during the winter months. Rates are generally lower in hotels and guest houses, too. You can actually walk down Duval Street and not bump into people. It feels like a real town, not just a tourist resort.

Locals say the best, most consistent weather is in March and April, with fewer thunderstorms and less intense heat. November and December are also idyllic and not so humid.

Although the Keys are casual and shorts are acceptable attire almost everywhere, one must take precautions against the ever-present sun. Wearing sunscreen, sunglasses, and perhaps a hat, particularly during the summer months, is highly recommended. Many locals wear long pants and light, long-sleeved shirts. I've often thought that dressing like a native of India, in loose, paper-thin white cotton or linen, would make sense here. You'll often need rain gear, a change of dry shoes, and a sweater or jacket for those winter months. But perhaps your most useful item of clothing is a bathing suit—the smaller, the better.

## Getting There

Only one route will take you into the Keys, Route 1 south, also known as the Overseas Highway. You can pick it up from the Florida Turnpike (Route 95) south of Miami and drive directly to Key West. The drive is spectacularly beautiful once you're outside the Miami suburbs and near the Everglades. But, for several reasons, I don't recommend driving down from Miami. For one thing, to get to Key West takes approximately four hours, more than most travelers expect. Although the distance is only 161 miles, Route 1 is not a fast road. It's often quite busy, and many sightseers are in no hurry. Trucks stop and start frequently. If you get held up at the drawbridge just above Key Largo, your voyage may take another hour. And you want to get to the Keys!

If you're going only as far as Key Largo, first in the chain of islands, you will need a vehicle. Rent a car at the Miami airport and head on out. Although Miami is a lush pastel-hued city and North Beach is worth exploring for its art deco hotels and long, white beaches, I can't recommend spending much time in the area. Airport car-rental agents will tell you to keep your car doors locked at all times. Miami is the first place I've seen people driving with handguns in their pockets. The city has much to be proud of in its natural and architectural beauty, but if you're headed to the Keys, get on with it.

After leaving the Miami suburbs, along which are scattered various fast-food restaurants (I'd eat at one of these because there are not as many choices on the highway for a stretch after Homestead), you'll arrive first in Homestead. The town has come a long way but is still rebuilding after the devastation of Hurricane Andrew in 1992. For the first year after that disastrous autumn, the entire area looked like a war zone. Much will perhaps never look the same, but the houses, hotels, and motels are almost all repaired. Along the road, you will often see farmers selling grapefruit and tomatoes from the backs of trucks.

Although you don't actually drive into the Everglades on Route 1, they surround you. Various side roads will take you into the Everglades National Park. The visitor center and park headquarters are just south of Florida City, which is just south of Homestead. At this point, you'll begin to see small, green "mile marker" signs along the highway's shoulder. These are placed at one-mile intervals and are the way locals give directions. For example, Key Deer Boulevard, which takes you to the Key Deer Refuge in Big Pine Key, is MM 30.5. Locals will also refer to "bay side" or "ocean side" after this MM direction. As you head south, the Atlantic Ocean is on your left, Florida Bay on your right.

Next stop is Key Largo, at which point you begin to be almost constantly bordered on two sides by water for the rest of your trip. The Keys are islands, after all, connected by this massive national highway and a series of bridges. Keep your eyes open for huge osprey nests atop power poles.

If your destination is either Marathon or Key West, I wouldn't drive at all. Marathon has an airport, in the process of being expanded, with daily flights in and out from all over Florida. Key West's larger, charming international airport has the ubiquitous ceiling fans and a pretty decent bar. Flights arrive and depart from most airports in Florida and from exotic islands farther out. One day soon perhaps you will be able to fly to Cuba from here.

If you decide to drive between Marathon and Key West, the most spectacular scenery begins around the astonishing Seven-Mile Bridge. If you haven't seen the ocean this far south, you're in for a visual treat. The blues are remarkable, and the comical, large brown pelicans and preening cormorants along the railings will charm you.

If your destination is Key West, a car is not necessary. The streets are already crowded, and many are but lanes. Key West is only two by four miles in its entirety, and you can easily walk around Old Town and parts of New Town. If you want to get out onto Roosevelt Boulevard, to see Houseboat Row or visit WaldenBooks, you can rent an inexpensive scooter or bicycle by the day or week. Plenty of nature is alive and well in the middle of town, even within the busiest neighborhoods. Twenty percent of the island's citizens don't own cars, and if you want to be mistaken for a local, do as they do: walk.

## Florida State Park Passes

If you are visiting the Keys for a considerable length of time, the Florida state park system offers two Real Florida Vacation passes. The Family Entrance Permit admits up to eight persons in the same vehicle and is valid for 15 days from the date of purchase; it costs $20.00. The Family Special Recreational Permit admits up to four persons in the same vehicle for special recreational activities (diving, boating, etc.) and up to eight persons in the same vehicle for entrance only. This pass, also valid for 15 days from date of purchase, is $25.00. Call 904-488-9872 for information.

## Camping Sites Throughout the Keys

The following is a partial list of the most popular and beautiful camping sites throughout the Keys, from north to south. Be sure to reserve well in advance, especially in the winter months, as they fill up quickly, particularly in the lower Keys where lodging prices are quite high. For the state parks, make reservations by phone, not by mail. They allow a two-week maximum stay.

- John Pennekamp Coral Reef State Park (see Index), MM 103, Key Largo. Call 305-451-1621.
- Florida Keys RV Resort. A Good Sam "approved" resort.

One hundred thirty-nine shaded campsites; fishing and boating nearby. Heated swimming pool, heated Jacuzzi. Pets welcome on leash. 106003 Overseas Highway, Key Largo. Call 305-451-6090.

- Long Key State Recreation Area (see Index), MM 67.5, Long Key. Call 305-664-4815.
- Sunshine Key RV Camping Resort and Marina. Four hundred sites from rental units to full hookup for RVs to tent camping. Some waterfront, at much higher rates. The resort does not guarantee specific site numbers. All amenities, including tennis and basketball courts, outdoor theater, and swimming pool. Daily reef trips; kayak rentals. Dog kennel and walks. Popular with families. Bay side. MM 39, Big Pine Key. Call 305-872-2217 or 800-852-0348.
- Bahia Honda State Park (see Index), MM 39, Bahia Honda. Call 305-872-3897.
- Fort Jefferson, on Garden Keys in the Dry Tortugas (see Index). The most primitive camping. Call 305-292-5201 (Key West Air Service) or 305-294-7009 (ferry).

## Popular Diving and Snorkeling Spots

The following sites are arranged from north to south, from Key Largo to Key West and the Dry Tortugas. All are reachable by boat. Many are extremely accessible; others a bit harder to reach. They range in difficulty from easy for beginners to safe only for advanced divers.

**Key Largo Dry Rocks.** The site of the underwater *Christ of the Deep* statue. (See John Pennekamp Coral Reef State Park entry on page 5.) The depth of the site is from 15 to 25 feet. The statue is marked by a spar buoy.

**The Benwood.** A wreck of a 285-foot freighter, which accidentally rammed the reef while running without lights during World War II. Huge grouper also live here. Ranges in depth from 35 to 50 feet. A great photography opportunity.

**French Reef.** A maze of underwater canyons, cliffs, and gullies. Popular with grouper and green moray eels.

**Molasses Reef.** A maze of coral channels and canyons, populated with a wide diversity of ocean life. Visibility is superior. Depths range from 25 to 40 feet.

**Hens and Chickens.** A shallow reef, 5 to 25 feet, about two miles off Islamorada. A fun shallow dive, perfect for snorkeling. A popular hangout for barracuda.

**The Eagle.** A vessel intentionally sunk as an artificial reef. You first encounter the superstructure at about 70 to 75 feet. Currents are strong; be extra cautious.

**Alligator Reef.** About 3.5 nautical miles southeast of Upper Matecumbe Key. Depths from 12 to 60 feet. Easily accessible; mooring buoys in place.

**Coffins Patch.** Several reefs, about four miles south-southeast of Key Colony Beach. A minimum depth of 7 feet, a maximum of about 25.

**West Turtle Shoals.** On the corner of Coffins Patch. The entire Coffins Patch is the only place where pillar coral grows in the middle Keys. Popular as a "no-take" area. ("No-take"

means divers may take photographs but no "souvenirs.")
Mooring buoys available throughout the entire patch; maximum depth about 20 feet.

**Lobster Ledge.** A favorite spot for the Florida spiny lobster and also for lobster fishing. A minimum depth of 12 feet; 300 feet west of Pillar Patch.

**The Stake.** Part of the Coffins Patch group of sites. Depths from 7 to 25 feet. Named for an iron pipe stake that juts out of the water, a remnant of a lighthouse downed in the 1935 hurricane.

**Pillar Patch.** About 11 miles east of the Stake. Has the largest colony of pillar coral in the area. These look like desert cactus and are great to photograph. No mooring buoys here.

**Yellow Rocks.** A system of older coral formation about four miles south of Key Colony Beach. Twenty-five feet deep; one of the largest reef systems in this area. Thousands of small fish—and some larger ones, including barracuda and nurse sharks—and invertebrates.

**The Thunderbolt.** Previously open only to wreck divers, the site has been made diver safe. The doors and hatches were removed, leaving "swim throughs" with the exit in sight. Best for divers with advanced certificates, primarily because of the current. Situated in 120 feet of water, this research vessel lies upright 230 feet below the surface on the Atlantic side of Marathon.

**Sombrero Light.** About four miles off Marathon's shore; easily spotted by the antique Sombrero Reef Light tower, which is visible for miles. The main reef area off Marathon. Twenty-five foot depths, with a "spur-and-groove" reef system. Coral finger is the "spur"; parallel channels of reef in four-foot shallows are the "grooves."

**Bahia Honda.** Good diving, but beware fast currents and abrupt tide changes. (See Index.)

**Looe Key National Marine Sanctuary.** Off Ramrod Key, about five nautical miles south of Big Pine Key. Considered by many experienced divers and snorkelers to be the most spectacular reef in the lower Keys. The remains of the *H.M.S. Looe*, which sank in 1744, lie within the sanctuary boundaries. There are also 39 buoys and a cave. Great for snorkeling and diving; has significant "spur-and-groove" systems.

**The Cayman Salvager.** A 180-foot steel-hulled buoy tender, sunk as an artificial reef in 1985, righted by hurricane-force wave action. Now in 65 to 90 feet of water on a sandy bottom. Recently was home to a 200-pound jewfish and a six-foot green moray eel.

**Kedge Lodge Reef.** No markers, so not often visited. Three 19th-century schooner anchors mark the 30-foot-deep area, near Key West.

**Joe's Tug.** A 75-foot steel-hulled tugboat in 55 to 65 feet near Key West. Sunk as an artificial reef in 1984. Lots of jewfish and moray eels.

**Nine Foot Stake.** Named for a stake protruding out of the water. About 20 feet deep; excellent spot for photography. Spur-and-groove coral, including six-foot-diameter brain coral and remains of a small lighthouse. Also barracuda and southern sting rays.

**Trinity Cove.** West of Key West, marks the beginning of the Boca Grande Bar. Forty-five- to 60-foot depths. Visibility averages 50 to 100 feet.

**Dry Tortugas.** Excellent snorkeling around the fort moats and on adjacent Loggerhead Key reefs. (See Index.)

For more information and a map, check out the Florida Keys website: Best of the Florida Keys at http://islandfun .com/. Look under Florida Keys Internet Guide, diving. Jim Shonborn at the Diving Site in Marathon is also a knowledgeable contact.

## Some Cautionary Notes

While you're enjoying the Keys, there are certains things you need to be aware of:

- Never swim after dark in the Keys. That's the time when sharks are most active. In fact, never swim when you see these carnivorous creatures. Do not swim or dive alone. Don't swim when bleeding and, of course, never molest or provoke a shark, even a small one. Most are not dangerous to humans, but why take a chance?
- Yes, it's true what you've heard: the mosquitoes throughout the Keys are large and swarming. From June to November are the most ferocious months because this is the wet season. Generally, from December to May, there are many fewer mosquitoes because the air is dry enough to stop them from hatching, and cold fronts (50 or 60 degrees) can kill the adult insects.
- Beware of fire ants. These bright red ants, accidentally introduced into Alabama from Brazil in the 1920s, now

exist throughout the South. The ants are minuscule, less than one-eighth of an inch long. You generally don't see them unless you step on their mound, a pile of dirt between 6 and 12 inches, usually found in a disturbed area, like on the side of a road. If these critters sting you, you will have itchy, raised pustules that may last for weeks.

- The sun, one of the main attractions of the Keys, is incredibly strong and quite seductive. The sun shines almost every day of the year, at least for half the day. Of course, you ought to be careful how much sun you expose your body to. Locals use sunscreen or sunblock or protect themselves with long sleeves and long pants most of the year. Sunglasses that block ultraviolet rays are recommended as well. You can generally tell the tourists because their skin is the darkest brown or the reddest. If you are swimming, boating, or even wading through water, you get a double amount of sun because the rays reflect off the water. There is a high incidence of skin cancer in Florida; don't take chances.

- Feeding alligators is not advised. Alligators are generally not harmful, but once they get a taste of human food, they like it. Although they appear lazy, they can react with great speed when provoked and have been known on rare occasions to maim or kill swimmers or small children playing near marshy areas. They also seem to favor the flavor of dog, so keep Fifi or Spot far away from any alligator pond or sinkhole.

- Several poisonous plants exist in the Keys. Three are particularly evident. Now on Florida's endangered species list, the native manchineel stands up to 30 feet and has shiny alternate leaves two to four inches long with slightly round-toothed margins and pointed tips. The sap is extremely irritating and its fruit, which looks like a small green crab apple, can be fatal. Many of these trees have been destroyed, but you can occasionally find them where you least expect. The second plant to watch out for is called the Florida poisontree or poisonwood. This tree is much more widespread than the manchineel. It grows in both wet and dry habitats, along roadsides, and in hammocks, pinelands, and coastal regions. The tree has alternate compound leaves with five shiny, yellow-edged, tiny leaves and black sticky stains on its bark and leaves. It grows a poisonous greenish-orange fruit. The third plant to beware of is the familiar three-leafed, shiny poison ivy, in its climbing form. You may see it anywhere in the Keys.

- Yes, indeed, there are snakes, although I have only seen one small black fellow, who scurried away. Four types of poisonous snakes exist in South Florida. These are the eastern diamondback rattler, the dusky pygmy rattler, the Florida cottonmouth (or water moccasin), and the eastern coral snake. The largest is the diamondback, which grows to eight feet and is named for its beautiful markings. The most poisonous are the pygmy rattlesnakes, which like to warm themselves on paved roads. Less than two feet long, their rattles are tiny and barely audible. Again, you're not likely to see any of these reptiles.
- Another creature you will probably never encounter is the scorpion. The Florida variety, which looks something like a tiny lobster, is not fatally poisonous, but the sting can make you sick. If you turn over a piece of wood, don't use your bare hands. Scorpions prefer hiding under fallen trees to hiding under rocks. If you do pick up wood, put it back as you found it, so no tiny creatures are left homeless.
- The jellyfish called Portuguese man-of-wars look beautiful, like iridescent blue balloons, but they can sting like

wasps. They have a clump of fine tentacles, sometimes 30 feet long. You may see them in the water, either floating or just under the surface. Give them a wide berth. They seem to arrive in spells, so you may never see them. You can usually apply home remedies for their sting, but some sensitive individuals may require a trip to the emergency room.

- Two varieties of rays exist in the Keys. These are odd-looking creatures that lie on the bottom of seas, bays, or rivers. Because its flat body with a long, sinewy tail is partly concealed by sand or mud, the ray is hard to see. These fish do not intentionally attack and will often swim to deep water if several bathers are in their area. However, if you inadvertently step on one, it will flip its tail up and around and drive its saw-toothed spine into your leg or foot. This causes pain, swelling, dizziness, and more. If this happens, call a doctor or use first aid as you would for a snakebite. You can help avoid stings by wearing shoes when walking in shallow water at the ocean's edge, by shuffling your feet as you walk, and by avoiding the beach when rays are reported out in force.

# Endangered Species in the Coral Reef Ecosystem

The following currently appear on the endangered species list.

**American crocodile.** Differences from the more common alligator include gray skin, a thinner body, and a narrow, pointed snout. Afraid of humans and prefers saltier water than alligators. There are only between 200 and 400 left.

**Arctic peregrine falcon.** A large bird with a dark cap and long pointed wings, often seen in the Keys during October and into the winter months.

**Atlantic green turtle.** Fairly small, between 36- and 43-inch shell length. Weighs between 300 and 350 pounds. Olive-brown shell with mottled streaks and spots.

**Atlantic ridley sea turtle.** The smallest of the five sea turtles here. Also the most endangered with fewer than 700 adult females as of 1994. Olive-gray carapace with a yellowish plastron. Ranges from 24 to 30 inches in shell length and weighs between 75 and 100 pounds.

**Grasshopper sparrow.** This subspecies is approximately four and a half inches long with a stripe on its upper part. Darker than most sparrows. Seen from mid-October to early May.

**Hawksbill sea turtle.** This turtle is endangered throughout the world; numbers unknown. Still a trade in it for tortoiseshell jewelry. It has a 30- to 36-inch shell length, and weighs between 100 and 200 pounds. It is colorfully marked and has thick, overlapping scales.

**Key deer.** Only approximately 500 to 600 of these tiny white-tailed deer live on and near Big Pine Key. This is their only habitat in the world. Threats include automobiles, running dogs, and overdevelopment of their habitat.

**Key Largo cotton mouse.** A tiny mouse found almost exclusively in hardwood hammocks of Key Largo.

**Key Largo wood rat.** Agile, rather docile rat found in hardwood hammocks of Key Largo. They collect brightly colored items to incorporate into their nests.

**Key mud turtle.** Found in hardwood hammocks in lower Keys. Live in fresh to brackish ponds, not salt water.

**Leatherback sea turtle.** Has four- to eight-foot shell length and weighs up to 2,000 pounds. This large sea turtle (the largest living species of turtle) has a rubbery, smooth, scaleless back, with a gray shell. It nests between April and November, between 9:00 P.M. and midnight. It is still hunted for its oils of cosmetic value and its prized eggs.

**Lower Keys marsh rabbit.** A subspecies of the marsh rabbit. Nocturnal and shy. Found from Big Pine Key to Boca Chica. Only 200 to 400 in wild, nearing extinction due to loss of habitat.

**Schaus swallowtail butterfly.** A large, dark brown swallowtail, a subspecies of the giant swallowtail but slightly smaller. Has bold yellow markings. Named by Miami collector William Schaus. Now found only in upper Keys and on a few islands in Biscayne National Park.

**Silver rice rat.** It is found on 9 or 10 of the lower Keys. An aquatic relative of the wood rat and the cotton mouse, once thought to be extinct.

**Stock Island tree snail.** This tiny, slithering gastropod is now mostly lives in captivity. As of 1994, only 450 existed. The governor's plum, a thorny tree which produces an edible fruit, is a host tree for this snail.

**West Indian manatee.** One of two subspecies of West Indian manatee. A gentle vegetarian mammal, weighing up to 3,500 pounds. The female is larger. In January 1996, the manatee numbered between 1,800 and 2,274 in Florida. Motorboats are its primary enemy.

**Woodstork.** The only stork native to North America. Approximately 5,000 alive. Between 35 and 47 inches tall, not including legs. A white and black bird with a naked head. This is the most endangered wading bird in Florida.

Fourteen other species, including several snakes and birds, are on the threatened species list. Additionally, several trees and flowering plants are on both lists.

# 1

# The Upper Keys

## Key Largo

Key Largo is the first and the largest of the Florida Keys, about 30 miles in length, from MM 110 to MM 87. Key Largo actually includes the settlements of Key Largo, Tavernier, and Plantation Key.

It was named Cayo Largo, "long island," by Spanish settlers. But, of course, many of us think of the famous Bogart and Bacall classic *Key Largo* when we hear the words *Key Largo*. Some scenes for the 1948 film were shot in the Upper Keys. (Speaking of Humphrey Bogart, you can see the original *African Queen* at MM 100; see entry on page 11).

The area is most known as a fishing and diving haven. The nation's first underwater park, John Pennekamp Coral Reef State Park (see on page 5), is here as is the adjacent Key Largo National Marine Sanctuary. Together, these consist of approximately 190 miles of reefs, sea-grass beds, and mangroves. Fifty-five types of coral and more than six hundred species of fish, a myriad of shore birds, and other wildlife exist in Key Largo.

The Upper Keys is a good place to find more reasonable prices than in the Lower Keys. Spend a few nights; do some souvenir shopping; get the feel for the water, vegetation, and wildlife of the Keys; and begin to "get sand in yours shoes," as you undoubedly will.

# Tavernier

There are two theories about the naming of Tavernier: one is that it is named for the drinking establishments which were popular with the Keys' ship "wreckers," of the 19th century; the other is that it is named for a small key offshore that the Spaniards had named "Cayo Tabona," or Horsefly Key. Tavernier is actually located in the larger area of Key Largo, although it does have its own town center.

The town's historic district contains more than 50 buildings from the early 1900s, including railroad stations, churches, homes, a school, and stores. The town also boasts a small shopping center and a movie theater, rare in the Keys. It and Plantation Key (south of Tavernier) are made up of 3,374 acres; they have a different zip code than the town of Key Largo, and their own schools.

# In Touch with Nature, Inc.

In Touch with Nature, Inc., is a Miami-based natural history tour operator made up of a father and daughter team. Wil Gilbert is a former biology, geology, and environmental science professor who retired after 31 years at Miami-Dade Community College; his daughter, Nancy, holds a degree in biology, and now has a company that trains animals—mostly dogs—for TV commercials and movies. In the past, she has trained animals ranging from clouded leopards to wolves to parrots. Wil is also a former board member of the Tropical Audubon Society, a branch of the national organization.

"Between us, we know all that needs to be known about our novel South Florida environment," says Wil Gilbert.

What the Gilberts offer is small, customized group or individual tours. They always take into consideration what their clients want to do; they have no memorized, scripted lectures. They discuss the itinerary together and, if the customers wish, modify it as they go through the day. The tours might involve birding, canoeing, wildlife photography, or swimming with dolphins. They can customize one day, two days, or more, based on individual client needs. They also provide multimedia presentations on the natural history of South Florida and lead seminars on environmental problems. They are available for seminars, conferences, workshops, or school talks.

Some of their trips fall into more of the straight sightseeing category, but what Wil and Nancy Gilbert prefer is to show the geology, flora, and fauna of the Keys. They do this by seven-passenger van and/or on foot; they are not boat-based. Originating in Miami, the father and daughter team go as far south as Key West. Fees are reasonable by industry standards, and there's a much lower rate for those under 10 years of age. Wil can negotiate fees for a group or large family. Fees include entrance to parks (not including alligator farms or Indian villages in the Miami and Everglades area). Airboat rides are often included and discounted. For your fee, you also receive a healthy picnic of cheese, bread, fruit, raw veggies, etc. Bottled water and snacks are available throughout the day. Their van is equipped with a spotting scope, several pairs of binoculars, and many books on South Florida fauna and flora.

Places they might explore include the Seven-Mile Bridge, the old Flagler railroad, Pigeon Key, or Key West. Sometimes they also go to see the Key deer. Explains Wil, "I don't think the little deer should be molested, but if we do get sight of them, it's good for another environmental lecture."

The Gilberts pick up clients at their hotel at whatever time they choose and return them at the end of the day. As he puts it, "If we have had a dissatisfied client, I don't know about it."

*For more information:* In Touch with Nature, Inc., 18921 N.W. 11th Avenue, Miami, FL 33169. Call 305-653-1139. Website: http://www.Geocities.com/yosemite/rapids/3379.

# Jules' Undersea Lodge

Although this is not a bed-and-breakfast guidebook, the unique Jules' Undersea Lodge has to be included because of its spectacular location and its views of reefs and sea creatures. Its windows and yard are some of the best places to see nature in the upper Keys.

Jules' Undersea Lodge, the only such accommodation in the world, is indeed underwater in a natural mangrove lagoon in Key Largo. It sits in 30 feet of water, and shares space with Marine Lab, an underwater research and educational lab. The principal developers of the project, Neil Monney and Ian Koblick, former aquanauts, named their undersea retreat for Jules Verne, author of *Twenty Thousand Leagues Under the Sea.* Guests, most of whom are certified divers, must descend five fathoms (30 feet) to enter their airtight rooms. If you're a newcomer to these water sports, introductory scuba courses are offered before you head to your submerged, yet dry, quarters. This is not an activity for the fearful or claustrophobic.

Once guests check in on land, they are shown a multimedia presentation, "The History of Man in the Sea." They then receive a tour of the operations and communication center, pack their luggage into watertight cases, and are escorted down to their rooms. The hotel stands approximately eight feet off the bottom of the lagoon, with a four-by-six-foot opening in its floor for entry. Guests dive with a continuous air supply from 120-foot hookah lines.

The rooms have 42-inch porthole windows with spectacular views of brilliantly striped fish and coral reefs, TVs and

VCRs, outside telephone communications, bathrooms and showers, and there's a galley setup for gourmet dining. The hotel, with approximately 600 square feet of living space, can accommodate six guests at one time. Staff is always available. As you might expect, room prices are in the luxury category; you're paying for the experience. Despite the high costs, rooms are often booked months in advance.

If you can't afford the overnight rate, the lodge also offers a much more reasonable Mini-Adventure Day Visit, during which you spend three hours diving, exploring, and visiting the lodge. The lodge is also available for underwater weddings!

If you choose to go to Jules', a few strict rules apply. Overnight guests cannot fly for 24 hours after surfacing. They cannot dive for 12 hours after surfacing, and from then until 24 hours after surfacing, they cannot dive deeper than 30 feet, the same depth as the hotel.

Divers can also see Marine Lab, the affiliated research laboratory owned by the Marine Resources Development Foundation, where scientists and students perform underwater research projects, and can visit an underwater classroom for shipwreck archaeology.

The lodge is an hour's drive from the Miami International Airport at MM 103.2 on the Overseas Highway.

*For more information:* Jules' Undersea Lodge, 51 Shoreland Drive, Key Largo, FL 33037. Call 305-451-2353 seven days a week between 9:00 A.M. and 3:00 P.M.

# John Pennekamp Coral Reef State Park

Established in 1960, the world-famous John Pennekamp Coral Reef State Park in Key Largo is named for journalist John

Pennekamp (1897–1978), associate editor and an environmental writer for the *Miami Herald*. He was also first chairman of the Florida Board of Parks and Historic Memorials, and was instrumental in the establishment of the Everglades National Park.

The nation's first underwater park, Pennekamp provides a base for offshore snorkeling, diving, glass-bottom boat trips, and more. It covers 178 nautical squares of coral reefs. It's home to Jules' Undersea Lodge (see previous entry) and to many above-ground activities.

As you head north, on your right, or ocean, side, you will see two entrances. Enter either and proceed to the tollbooth. The visitor center is open 8:00 A.M. to 5:00 P.M. Start there. Facilities include a snack bar and well-stocked gift shop, as well as a bathhouse and rest rooms with outdoor showers. The center also has nature videos for viewing in a theater room. Behind these buildings is a high wooden observation deck. In this entry area are lots of sheltered tables and benches and clear signage giving directions for various places within the large park and announcements of activities for the day. Signs everywhere ask you to please limit water usage. You'll see these throughout the Keys. Water for drinking and bathing is expensive here; it's brought down by pipe from the mainland.

An excellent 30,000-gallon saltwater aquarium in the visitor center is well labeled and contains good displays on local habitats such as the sea-grass community. There are also displays on the spiny lobster, animals of the hammock, including the endangered Key Largo wood rat, and more. It contains an excellent, detailed display of stony and soft corals as well.

If you prefer to stay on dry land, trails can take you through part of the park. The five-minute Mangrove Trail goes over a boardwalk and is accessible to the disabled. You walk over a tidal creek, a natural channel like a river, with lots of fish. This is also an excellent spot in which to canoe or kayak. An observation deck lets you look into the thick mangroves, and, as is true throughout the park, signage is clear. Be aware that during midday, it's very hot and you'll see no birds. A few of the animals you might see, at other times of the day, include opossum, deer, raccoon, and fiddler crabs.

A longer trail, to the right of the visitor center, is the Wild Tamarind Nature Trail, which takes about 20 minutes to complete. This winds through a tropical hardwood hammock. Big pieces of coral line the path; there is generally a breeze and a few benches on which to take a rest. I've seen lots of lizards and skinks scurrying on the ground and trees here. Also, I saw a two- or three-foot black snake with white under its chin. Always look down as well as up. Guided walks on both these paths are offered seasonally or upon request.

But most people come here for the water. Popular are small-craft boating, canoeing, and kayaking on ocean trails through dense overhanging mangroves. Snorkeling, sailing, and scuba tours are available. Snorkeling and scuba gear, canoes, kayaks, rafts, bumper boats, and more can be rented for a reasonable price. The park also offers many diving trips and programs, some leading to certification.

The park offers nine diving sites, each with a particular personality. The largest snorkeling reef is White Bank Dry Rocks. The most unusual is Key Largo Dry Rocks, site of the famous nine-foot, 4,000-pound bronze statue, *Christ of the Deep*. People even get married here. This is a duplicate of the *Christ of the Abysses* statue in the Mediterranean near Genoa, Italy. Donated to the park by an Italian fisherman, it is made of bronze and was placed here in 20 feet of water.

A glass-bottom boat, the *San Jose*, departs three times a day and makes a two-and-a-half-hour trip through South Sound Creek and out to Molasses Reef, the only reef it visits. Unfortunately, it does not include a view of the *Christ* statue.

Try to take any glass-bottom boat trip on a calm day. If you're in the least prone to seasickness, be aware that the boat does bounce around, and while you're on board you might experience some unpleasant moments. You will certainly see lots of fish and some coral, but not necessarily sharks, turtles, or shy reef residents.

A sandy beach and 47 full-facility camping sites are also in the park. Swimming is possible at Cannon Beach and two other areas. Reservations for campsites are recommended; they must be made by phone or in person. No pets are allowed on the camping sites. Other forbidden objects and activities in the park include alcohol, spear fishing, firearms, and fireworks.

You can't miss the park. At MM 102.5 ocean side, it's advertised up and down the Keys on large billboards. It is 25 miles south of Homestead, and 60 miles from Miami International Airport.

*For more information:* John Pennekamp Coral Reef State Park, MM 102.5, P.O. Box 487, Key Largo, FL 33037. Call 305-451-1202. Website: http://pennekamppark.com/.

# The Coral Reef

The coral reef is the most spectacular, and perhaps the most threatened, of the natural wonders of the Florida Keys. In *The Enchanted Braid, Coming to Terms with Nature on the Coral Reef,* author Osha Gray Davidson calls reefs "the very soul of the sea." The only living coral reef in the contiguous United States, this is the third largest in the world. In fact, the Florida Keys is the world's top destination for amateur snorkelers and divers. It adds millions of dollars annually to the local economy; that's a lot of people using the reef. Located on the ocean side of the islands about six miles offshore and paralleling the Keys (for approximately 158 miles), this barrier reef is more than 5,000 years old.

What exactly is a coral reef? Good question—which many people don't know how to answer. Coral is a soft living organism, called a polyp, which secretes a skeleton of calcium carbonate. It is closely related to a sea anemone. Some corals are solitary (one polyp), but most species form colonies composed of hundreds or thousands of polyps, which cover either a stony (hard) or soft skeleton. This living tissue forms a thin sheet of cells over the skeleton and measures less than one-sixteenth inch in thickness. The coral or polyps keep multiplying, eventually forming a reef.

Sixty-three species and subspecies of hard corals as well as 42 species of soft corals exist in the Keys. Hard corals secrete limestone and are the most prominent. Soft corals are more delicate and tend to grow in deeper waters. Some fragile corals only grow one inch in several years.

The reef's ecosystem includes sea grasses and a variety of mangroves (saltwater-tolerant trees with a clearly visible root system) that enhance the productivity of the reef ecosystem. More than 400 species of fish swim in the waters surrounding the reef.

Coral can be easily destroyed by a variety of things—nutrients from sewage, fertilizers, storm water runoff, and deteriorating water quality—causing increased incidence of coral diseases and algae blooms. Trash or monofilament line wrapped around the corals can smother or break them. Trash can also be deadly for birds, fish, and turtles that mistakenly eat it or become tangled in it.

Three kinds of coral diseases have been discovered in the Keys in the last few years: yellow blotch or yellow band; white plague type 2; and the newest, discovered in early 1997, a white pox which seems especially virulent. This disease spreads quickly and kills up to 70 to 80 percent of the coral it infects. According to another report, in Davidson's reef book, the following diseases have also been discovered here: black band disease, white plague type 1, and red bland. When James Porter, a zoologist at the University of Georgia, did a reef study in the Keys between 1984 and

1991, he found that five of his six sites had lost hard-coral cover at an average rate of about 5 percent per year.

In the hot, dry summer of 1998, the coral reef off the Florida Keys became bleached because of stress. This bleaching, which makes the reefs look white like snow, can slow growth and affect reproduction, as if the reefs didn't have enough stress already.

Of course, this beautiful reef is one of the main natural attractions of the Keys. But everyone must learn how to take better care of it so it will be here for future generations to enjoy and admire.

Here are a few helpful hints for divers, snorkelers, and boaters to better protect the fragile coral reef system:

- Avoid physical contact with coral if at all possible.
- Do not touch or stand on coral; this can badly damage the coral and its entire system.
- Avoid wearing gloves, if at all possible. People who wear gloves (or booties) often believe it's safer to touch coral with protective clothing. This is not so.
- Don't collect marine life. Most captured tropical fish die within a year. Conch, a large-shell mollusk, is a protected species, and harvesting coral in the Florida Keys is strictly prohibited.
- Don't feed the fish while you're diving or snorkeling.
- Bring your trash to shore and recycle it; it is illegal to dump trash at sea.
- Be careful where you anchor your boat; do not anchor over coral.
- Don't discharge bilgewater onto the reef. Large boats should use sewage pump-out facilities and biodegradable bilge cleaner.
- Take only pictures as your souvenirs.
- Don't buy coral products at local stores; harvesting coral depletes all fragile reefs.

# The *African Queen*

The *African Queen* is purely a nostalgia stop, but it's worth a few minutes and a postcard for Humphrey Bogart and Katharine Hepburn fans. Come on now, how many times have you seen the movie?

On the ocean-access canal next to the Key Largo Holiday Inn, the original boat, built in Lytham, England, in 1912 for service in Africa on the Victoria Nile and Lake Albert, is moored on free public display. The 30-foot-long boat, powered by a steam-combustion engine, has been around the world twice.

If you're feeling intrepid, you can actually take a cruise, by reservation. Or you can just recall the fabulous movie made in 1951 (filmed on Lake Albert), with its improbable and satisfying romance between two of the more incompatible characters ever seen on the screen.

The historic vessel is located at Holiday Inn Docks, MM 100, Key Largo.

*For more information:* Call 305-451-4655.


# Harry Harris County Park

An uncommercial, family-type, ocean-side beach and play area, Harry Harris County Park is located at MM 93, Burton Drive, in Tavernier. Harris, its namesake, was an early restaurateur and county commissioner who lived from 1904–1978. Aside from a small swimming area in a tidal pool, the park has playground equipment, tennis courts, a boat ramp, ball fields, shaded picnic tables, grills, and rest rooms. The beach is sandy, the water always calm. There are also signs warning of the possibility of Portuguese man-of-wars in the water, so watch those legs.

The park, for which there is an admission fee for nonresidents, is open from 8:00 A.M. to sundown. Dogs are not allowed. Look for signs on the Overseas Highway in Tavernier; the road winds around a residential area for about two miles before reaching the park.

## Florida Keys Wild Bird Center

Florida Keys Wild Bird Center is a terrific wild bird sanctuary in Key Largo where you will see many species you may not see elsewhere. Have you ever spotted a Wurdemann's heron or a least grebe? Unfortunately, many of them are ill or injured, but others are definitely on the mend and flying around. Also on the premises are two short nature trails. Like the Wildlife Rescue of the Florida Keys in Key West (see Index), the Wild Bird Center has licensed wildlife rehabilitators who work in conjunction with local veterinary clinics experienced in wildlife care. The primary goals of the center, which is larger than that in Key West, are the rescue, rehabilitation, and eventual release of ill, injured, and orphaned wild birds. Unlike the Key West site, this center houses only birds; it treats approximately 1,100 a year. The center, a nonprofit organization funded by donations, a gift shop, a newsletter, and special events, receives no federal or state money.

The center is divided into 20 habitats. You can look at the birds through many of the cages, or in some cases through two-way mirrors. Injured and sick birds do not take kindly to being stared at directly—prey species, especially, can become very stressed, which often causes severe health problems. In one of the screened-in "educational" habitats, you can walk among a large brood of flapping, injured brown pelicans (I discovered these pelicans can live to be 25) and a few gulls. Other birds often being treated include the great blue heron,

*Roseate Spoonbill*

cattle egret, Wurdemann's heron (a species only found in the Keys), pomarine yaeger, white-crowned pigeon, little green heron, roseate spoonbill (a species with about 500 breeding pairs throughout Florida), the magnificent frigate bird with its enormous wingspan of seven to eight feet, Eastern screech owl, various hawks, and many more. Most caged areas have signs offering information on the species and its habitat.

In the center's brochure is a section on loss of habitat, one of the primary issues threatening the health and numbers of Florida Keys bird populations. Between 1955 and 1985, for example, more than 40 percent of the shallow-water mangrove pools on the upper Florida Keys were lost to human development.

Once you've examined all the beautiful birds, you can take a 10-minute walk in a wetlands and salt-marsh area across the driveway from the caged-in areas. Trees, such as the Christmas berry tree (or shrub), called "the most toxic fruit in North America," which blossoms in winter, are clearly labeled. Also notable are the pigeon plum, a huge gumbo limbo, barbed-wire cactus, and wild lime. You may see several tiny spiders as well, including the fairly common crab spider, native to tropical and subtropical America. This tiny colorful creature has a hard abdomen armed with spines, hangs in the middle of its web, and is adorned with white tufts.

Behind the sanctuary, a shorter walk takes you to a boardwalk along the water, with benches and chairs on which to rest.

If you're moved by your visit to the Florida Keys Wild Bird Center and are staying in the area for a while, the staff is always looking for volunteer help. You can donate fish for the birds' diets, transport birds, or repair cages, among other efforts. The facility also runs a college internship program of about 15 weeks' duration. Interns live on the premises, work 40 hours a week, and help in all activities, including bird feeding (creatures like fish, crickets, and mealworms), intake, and cleaning. Admission is free but donations are, of course, eagerly accepted. The center's small gift shop carries an excellent selection of books, including an inclusive small book called *Birding in the Florida Keys*, and several prints, magnets, and the like. Soda machines and bathrooms are on the premises, but food is not available.

The Center is open to the public daily. A walk through the entire facility and the nature trails should take close to two hours. It is located on the Overseas Highway at MM 93.6, bay side. When you're on Route 1 in Key Largo, look for the wooden sign in the shape of a heron.

*For more information:* The Florida Keys Wild Bird Center 93600 Overseas Highway, Key Largo, FL 33037. Call or fax: 305-852-4486. Website: http://www.thefloridakeys.com/keylargo/bird.htm.

# Cowpens Key Audubon Sanctuary

Located at MM 90-B, Cowpens is a wild bird sanctuary, not open to the public, but the waters surrounding it are wonderful for kayaking or canoeing and wide enough for a small motorized boat. A waterway cuts through the mangrove, and there is a clear, restful mangrove creek running through the southwest corner of the key. The National Audubon Society acts as manager of the site, leased from the state of Florida.

Cowpens Key is named for manatees (sea cows), not cattle. At one time, there were so many manatees in this area that they were herded into these watery "pens" to await being caught and turned into meat. Of course, now that they're almost extinct, manatees are no longer eaten.

Cowpens is a mangrove island, about 30 years old, and about three-quarters of a mile off Plantation Key along Cross Bank (a big and long marl bank). The Audubon office is located at MM 90; Cowpens, which is only accessible by boat, is at the very edge of Everglades National Park. Jet skis are not allowed in the park.

Cowpens is important to the following birds for nighttime roosting: various herons, white-crowned pigeon, ground doves, and the occasional red-shouldered hawk. Magnificent frigate birds use it as a roost primarily in the spring and fall; they can be found on the mangrove clumps on the north side of the key.

These species and more use it as a nesting site: white-crowned pigeon, reddish egrets, prairie warblers, gray king-birds, clapper rails, and, as biologist Rick Sawicki puts it, "lots of mosquitoes." The beautiful and elegant roseate spoonbills used to use this key extensively as a nesting area, but they have mostly shifted to nesting farther north at Florida Bay. Sightings are still possible, usually during the winter.

# White-Crowned Pigeon

The white-crowned pigeon is another threatened species in South Florida; its exact numbers are unknown. In 1991, the breeding population here was thought to be 5,055 pairs. This pigeon is a Caribbean species, which nests in the United States only in South Florida and in the Keys. It also breeds in the Bahama Islands, the Greater Antilles, and the Lesser Antilles south to Antigua. In the Caribbean, this is a popular game bird.

The bird is gray, with a greenish neck and a white cap, stocky, about 13½ inches tall, and about the size and build of the more familiar urban pigeon. Its white cap is especially distinctive. These special pigeons feed on fruits of hardwood trees found in tropical forests; development greatly threatens their food base. According to a September 1994 article in the *Journal of Wildlife Management,* these pigeons are important to South Florida's ecosystem because when they feed they disperse seeds from more than 35 species of fruiting trees, shrubs, and vines.

In an article published in *Conservation Biology* in September 1994, Allan M. Strong and G. Thomas Bancroft of the National Audubon Society in Tavernier wrote, "White-crowned pigeons may play a pivotal or keystone role as seed dispersers in south Florida's ecosystem because of their mobility, fairly large population size, diet diversity, and tendency to pass most seed intact." They advise protecting large forest fragments on southern Key Largo for their refuge.

In the Keys, the birds live from the Marquesas Keys north to Elliott Key. They nest primarily on offshore, dense mangrove, uninhabited islands. The birds are monogamous, with males attending the nest during the day and females protecting it through the night. Both parents make daily flights to feed their young.

Potential nest predators for this rare pigeon include red-winged blackbirds, the American crow, the Virginia opossum, the bobcat, rats, and raccoons, which are multiplying in the Keys.

They may be seen almost anywhere in the Keys, especially during their nesting season, May through September. Expert birders have seen them early in the morning or late in the day at the John Pennekamp State Park, North Key Largo, Long Key State Park, and Big Pine Key. Flights of these pigeons have been observed over Mallory Dock in Key West. Another place to spot them, like the ospreys, is on the tops of trees or on electrical wires. Rick Sawicki, a scientist for Audubon in Tavernier, recommends power pole #222 on State Road 905 in Key Largo.

This is just one threatened species among many here in the Keys, but the white-crowned pigeon's ecological status reminds us that all species are interconnected. We cannot lose one without harming the others.

# Windley Key Fossil Reef State Geological Site

Windley Key Fossil Reef State Geological Site is one of seven state parks supported by the Friends of the Islamorada Area State Parks, a nonprofit group. This geological site is one of only two such state sites in Florida. It was purchased by the state in 1985 with money available through the Conservation and Recreation Lands program (CARL). Appeals by environmentalists, led by former Monroe County Commissioner Alison Fahrer of Windley Key, saved the geologically significant spot from being developed into a 156-condominium community.

Windley Key is the highest of the Keys, at a dazzling 16 feet above sea level. The site was laid down during an interglacial period about 125,000 years ago. The fossilized coral rock quarried here was called keystone.

A bit of history is in order. After Key West was first settled, "Conch" families moved up the Keys to begin farming and fishing. In the mid-1800s the Russell family homesteaded what was then called "Umbrella Keys" (two separate islands), Windley's earlier name. In 1908 the family sold their tract to the Flagler Florida East Coast Railway, and quarrying began. Until the completion of the Overseas Railroad, the quarries on the tract were used for the abutments for its bridges. Once the railroad was in operation, Quarry Station was a regular stop for passengers, for the delivery of fresh water from the mainland, and for the shipment of keystone to the mainland. When the railroad was destroyed in the 1935 hurricane, Quarry Station was also leveled but quarrying at the site continued.

The completion of the Overseas Highway in 1938 encouraged new quarrying of keystone, and the quarry was leased to several companies. The early 1960s was the last period of commercial quarrying. Rock from the quarry was used for the coral facades of the elaborate mansion, Vizcaya, in Miami, and the Miami and St. Louis, Missouri post offices. It has also been used locally for churches and homes.

Windley Key Fossil Reef State Geological Site consists of 32 acres. Five trails, with markers, can take you through the quarry areas, now split into Windley Quarry, Flagler Quarry, and Russell Quarry. The shortest is Quarry Walls Walk, in which you can stand inside a petrified coral reef. This is approximately 400 feet long. The longest is Hammock Trail Guide, approximately 2,680 feet long, which takes you through high hammocks, wetlands, and the transitional areas between them. In the coral quarry walls, you can see fossils of shells and marine creatures. According to Cesare Emiliani, former chairman of the Department of Geology at the University of Miami, it is the only place in the world where you can walk inside a coral reef and see how it is constructed. Many rock-cutting pieces of machinery and railroad ties on an old siding are also on-site. Each year, Windley Key attracts many geologists and college students.

Plans have been developed by the State Division of Recreation and Parks for a gatehouse, rest rooms, and an environmental education center at the site. Water and electrical facilities now exist, and the groundbreaking for the new Fahrer Education Center, named for Alison Fahrer, was held in late January 1998. The center, to be built with $350,000 from the Florida governor's 1997–98 operating budget, received unanimous approval in 1998 from both houses of the Florida legislature, and construction will probably be completed by the time you read this. The ground floor will consist of a display and exhibit area, with hands-on exhibits. The second floor will be a meeting and community room. Florida park rangers and volunteers will staff the facility, located at MM 85.5 bay side at the northern end of Islamorada.

As the park is only open occasionally, call for an appointment. The quarry also sponsors an annual open house and picnic in February or March.

*For more information:* Call 305-664-4815 (park manager) or the Friends of the Islamorada Area State Parks at 305-664-4704.

# Theater of the Sea

The Islamorada-based Theater of the Sea, begun in the 1940s, is the second oldest marine park in the country. This stop can easily keep a family or an individual busy for two to six hours. There's lots to do, food available, and several educational opportunities. You will know you've arrived because of the large highway sign on Route 1 and because of the large topiary dolphins, which give you some indication of what you'll find here.

But Theater of the Sea does more than house and train dolphins. You'll also see dozens of species of fish, sharks, sea lions, hermit crabs, sea anemones, and much more. Some of these slippery critters are even in touch tanks, always a popular activity with children or the child in us all.

The admission is a bit steep, but you get your money's worth. However, be on the lookout for coupons in tourist newspapers or brochures.

One of the first things I noticed on my most recent guided tour were several signs reading "Please don't handle or feed the cats." Cats? Is this an animal refuge? Yes and no. The center houses approximately 50 cats, part of the huge population of almost-feral and abandoned cats in the Keys. Admire, but don't pet.

Our first stop was to see dangerous sharks, sport fish, and game fish. The sport fish come to this facility when people release them. Among them are six-foot, 200-pound tarpon that are great gymnasts. Also on display are bonefish (strong fighters), barracuda (not very aggressive but curious, with large teeth), groupers, snooks, and on and on. Luckily, there's no quiz on naming species.

The next stop was the turtle tank. Did you know sea turtles can stay underwater for 48 hours? Lucy, a loggerhead that was hit by a boat propeller, is blind in one eye and may have some brain damage. You'll also find a hawksbill; the species, which has been used for tortoiseshell jewelry, is not internationally protected but is protected in the Keys. Other specimens include a Kemp's ridley turtle. After the turtles, we look toward the sky to see the raptors in large comfortable-looking netted pens; these include barred owls, red-tailed hawks, and a great-horned owl.

The ray tanks hold both the spotted eagle ray, which can jump 10 feet out of the water (the female gives birth to the baby in the air); and the southern ray, which stings people when they step on its barbed tail. This can cause nausea or temporary paralysis, so look for warning signs on beaches. They prefer shallow, sandy areas and only sting if you step on their barb while they're nesting.

After seeing sharks, crocodiles, and six touch tanks full of smaller specimens, we were rounded up to attend one of several daily dolphin shows. These are held in a three-acre lagoon, 22 feet in depth. In 1997, the facility had 11 Atlantic bottlenose dolphins, 4 in each show. They seem well cared for and relatively happy; of course, dolphins do like human contact and like learning and performing tricks and routines. In this show, two of the creatures "sang," swam, and dove, but the focus was on education. The trainers spoke throughout the jumping and gymnastics, and no one clapped during the performance. As one trainer said, "They're an awesome responsibility, and we must all do our part."

Next up were two California sea lions, sisters Sassy and Classy, 14 and 13 years old, respectively. They hail from Aurora, Ohio, can walk on their back flippers, swim 15 to 20

MPH, and stay out of the water indefinitely. These creatures can live 30 to 40 years.

Both of these shows entail physical interaction with kids. The sea lions hug and kiss the kids, which, of course, is a wonderful photo opportunity, if not at all natural for the creatures.

Finally, we took a 10-minute trip in a small, glass-bottom boat in the lagoon, once a rock quarry dug out for the Flagler's famous failed railroad. We saw a few dolphins swim by and leap into the air, then returned to the entrance of the park, where there is a small, relatively well-stocked gift shop. One final attraction is a small aquarium, but not all species are labeled.

Another option available at Theater of the Sea is the "Trainer for a Day" program, which enables children 10 years and younger to participate in daily training sessions. You can also participate in a dolphin swim or observe a swim. Reservations are suggested for the trainer program, and required for the dolphin swims.

Given the opportunity, I'd rather see these creatures in the wild than in a captive environment. But the staff seems honestly loving toward the animals, and at least it's a place to learn about them before setting out into backcountry to find them on your own. This is one of the better marine parks I've seen. It is located at MM 84.5 on Route 1 on the right heading north, in Islamorada, and is open from 9:30 A.M. to 4:00 P.M.

*For more information:* Theater of the Sea, 84721 Overseas Highway, Islamorada, FL 33036. Call 503-664-2431.

# Rain Barrel Village

The Rain Barrel Village on Plantation Key at MM 86.7 on Route 1 is an unusual art gallery. I have included it for a couple of reasons. It has a lovely, small garden that has won a

Beautification Award from the Islamorada Chamber of Commerce. Many of the trees are labeled—including Jamaica dogwood, gumbo limbo (small, colorful trees like those at the Audubon House in Key West), and various succulents. And it's a cool, shady spot for a short midday break.

Inside the series of shops are the tasteful works of various craftspeople from Florida and a few other states, which include pottery, paintings, fabrics, stained glass, and jewelry. A sculpture gallery is on-site. Much of the art celebrates Florida's natural beauty. This is a mini indoor-outdoor bazaar with personality.

*For more information:* Rain Barrel Village, 86700 Overseas Highway, Islamorada, FL 33036. Call 305-852-3084.

# Hurricane Monument

At MM 81.5 in Islamorada, on the ocean side in a small park in the middle of two roads, you will see a large native coral statue with palm trees wildly blowing in the breeze around it. Its inscription reads, "Dedicated to the memory of the civilians and war veterans whose lives were lost in the hurricane of September second 1935." A WPA project, also called the Matecumbe Art Project, the Hurricane Monument was dedicated on November 14, 1937.

The damage inflicted by this force-five hurricane was immense. The Overseas Railroad disappeared. Seventeen-foot tidal waves buried everything and washed the island at Marathon bare. Between 500 and 600 bodies were recovered. Three camps of veterans were in the path of the hurricane; it obliterated a whole small settlement. The crypt of the monument contains the remains of some of those killed. Winds blew faster than 250 MPH. Surprisingly, Key West did not suffer much damage from the hurricane.

That was the last major hurricane to hit the Florida Keys. Each year, between mid-August and mid-October there is the potential of a hurricane—a huge storm with high winds and strong tides—but hurricanes seldom hit this far south. Sometimes residents board up their windows and fill their bathtubs with water, and they wait for the wild tempest. But even the deadly Hurricane Andrew of August 1992 only hit as far south as Homestead.

*Note: Islamorada* means "the Purple Isles," named centuries ago by Spanish explorers who had seen lavender shells of sea snails, called Janthina, in the surf. Indians lived on this group of islands nearly 4,000 years ago.

# Lignumvitae Key State Botanical Site

Located at MM 77.5 in Islamorada, Lignumvitae Key is only accessible by boat. This historic botanical site is part of the Florida State Park system. You buy your boat tickets at a shop behind Robbie's Hungry Tarpon, a restaurant and fishing business, which is the official ferry for this site. While you wait, you can watch dozens of tarpon floating in the water; you can even buy a pail of smaller fish to feed them if you choose. Be careful not to stick your hand in the water; some of these fish are six to seven feet long and mighty hungry.

Lignumvitae Key is isolated and uninhabited, except for a caretaker. The total protected acreage on both Lignumvitae Key and nearby Shell Key is more than 11,347 acres.

The day I took the tour in February, Melba Nezbed, one of four park rangers who oversees the two botanical sites (this and Indian Key), led our small group. Dressed in official park garb, she was extremely knowledgeable, professional, and friendly. She came to this job 19 years ago.

People visit this primarily as a botanical site, so Nezbed calls the 1919 Matheson House "icing on the cake." Once you arrive at the stone house, which marks the beginning of your tour, be sure to put on the free mosquito repellent. This is extremely buggy territory, even in off-season. In the house are displays of shells, artifacts of broken dishes and bottles, polished-wood samples, hawksbill turtle shells (collected before the turtles became protected), Seminole artifacts from Indian Key dating from early in the century, and old photos of the Overseas Railroad. Huge native sponges and a collection of old bottles are on display in the tiny bathroom that features a claw-foot tub. Cozy wicker chairs, oil lamps hanging on the walls, and a black-and-white Rosewood stove make this a homey, if remote, house.

Until 1972 the house was occupied by caretakers instead of its wealthy owners, the Mathesons. The last occupant lived in this remote, buggy place for 20 years. The sturdy house survived the 1935 hurricane; the roof popped off but some of the house remained and the rest was rebuilt. In the back of the house is an 18-inch-thick hurricane shelter, built after the 1935 hurricane, which, fortunately, has not been used.

The significance of the surrounding forest, explained Melba, is that it is a freshwater, tropical forest; it needs some elevation to be designated a freshwater forest. The larger and higher islands—Marathon, Key West, and Plantation Key—have these forests. On this island, 16.5 feet above sea level, 41 species of hardwoods, including lignum vitae, thrive. This hardwood is extremely heavy to hold; it sinks like stone. Lignum vitae is also very dense; one cubic foot weighs 88 pounds. It was used in World War II on wooden ships and for propeller shafts. It was made into bearings for submarines as it holds up well in salt water. Nezbed told us that these higher keys are the only place this hardwood grows in North America. Even the small lignum vitae trees, which resemble bonsai, are hundreds of years old. The blossom is a purple-blue color, visible beginning in March.

Also noteworthy in this forest are such species as sapodilla, a non-native tree that has an edible pearlike fruit and produces natural chickle that can be used for gum, prickly pear cactus, barbed wire cactus, gumbo limbo, poisonwood (a critical food source for the endangered white-crowned pigeon), strangler figs, and mastic fruit trees. The latter bear sticky sweet fruits especially beloved by raccoons.

Amazingly, the entire forest on Lignumvitae Key grew from bird droppings.

Raccoons are not the only creatures that live here. You might see herons, pelicans, and the occasional white-crowned pigeon, a marsh rabbit, a variety of snakes, the occasional cotton mouse, and a few of 40 different species of butterflies.

No pets, alcohol, drugs, or firearms are allowed on Lignumvitae Key. All plant and animal life is protected; take only photographs as souvenirs.

Our guide wouldn't recommend this tour in the summer months because of the mosquitoes. If February is any indication, I'd say she's right-on.

Tours are available Thursday through Monday; you must make a reservation. The maximum number allowed on the key at one time is 50—25 on the trails, 25 in the clearing. Wear walking shoes and sunscreen, bring something cool and refreshing to drink, and use their repellent or bring your own.

You'll see Robbie's on Route 1 at MM 77.5. It's just south of the village of Islamorada on the bay side.

*For more information:* Robbie's Hungry Tarpon, P.O. Box 1052, Islamorada, FL 30336. Call 305-664-4815, or for reservations, 305-664-9814.

# Hibiscus

The ubiquitous hibiscus, "the Queen of the Tropics," is every-where you look in the Florida Keys. For Northerners or Mid-westerners, the size of its blossoms and the height of the shrub is startling. Many of us can grow small hibiscus in pots indoors, but in the Keys these beauties are outdoors everywhere. What might grow 2 feet in New England may well grow 20 feet here, almost overnight! They prefer full sun, not a problem in the Florida Keys.

The Red Shawl Ladies, volunteers, present cruise-boat visitors with an open hibiscus as they disembark. This is an old custom. But red isn't the only color available throughout the Keys. There are hundreds of shades and varieties: pinks, whites, yellow, pur-ples, salmons, oranges, mixtures in single and double blossoms. The doubles do look somewhat like roses, or perhaps double petu-nias, but much, much larger. More than 200 species of the showy flower exist.

Hibiscus is a native of either southern China (it's often called Chinese hibiscus) or the Pacific islands. It is the official flower of Hawaii and the national flower of Malaysia, but it could well be the state flower here, too. In Hawaii, a wild white hibiscus grows. Its rel-atives (it's in the Malvaceae or mallow family) include rose of Sharon, okra, cotton, the Confederate rose, and others.

The hibiscus has been cultivated in Florida for around a cen-tury. In a 1995 lecture, hibiscus expert Joe Allen of the Key West Garden Club said the first hibiscus was introduced in Bradenton, Florida, in 1904. A Hawaiian hybridizer sent seeds to a gardener there.

Hibiscus names are almost as lovely as the flowers: Green Hor-net, Magician's Hat, Handsome Stranger, Holy Smoke, Eye of the Storm. It blooms year-round, but its showy and seductive blos-soms, often five to nine inches across, last only one day. Enjoy intensely a flower in a small vase; the next morning, it will be wilted. Exceptions include the Ruth Wilcox, a white hibiscus, and a few yellows on which the blossoms last two whole days. And in the more northern Everglades, blossoms often last half a day.

---

# Indian Key State Historic Site

Lignumvitae Key is not the only offshore historic key to explore in southeastern Florida. Indian Key State Historic Site, about 10 acres in size, is located about three-quarters of a mile southeast from the north shore of Lower Matecumbe Key (MM 77.5). Tour boats leave Robbie's Hungry Tarpon twice a day, Thursday through Monday, for this overgrown, historic place.

The history of this key dates from the time of prehistoric Indians; it has been uninhabited since the early 1900s. As you may know, Indians lived in the Keys for thousands of years before Spanish explorers arrived with Ponce de Leon's discovery of Florida in 1513.

The British briefly occupied Florida starting in 1763. By then, the Calusas Indians had disappeared. Bahamian fishermen and turtlers then inhabited the islands, and they made salvage or wrecking of ships their way of life. This was lucrative, and it also attracted pirates. The American occupation of Florida, beginning in 1821, stopped the pirates' activities. The American wreckers also drove the Bahamian wreckers out of business. Key West was at that time a wealthy community from the salvage profits.

One man, Jacob Housman, a transplant from Staten Island, challenged the monopoly of Key West's wreckers. Although he at first worked within the system, local wreckers accused him of shady business practices. So, he thought it best to begin his own wrecking station on Indian Key. He chose this location, in part, because it is very close to the most dangerous reefs in the Keys.

Housman bought the entire island in 1831 and built a store, hotel, dwellings with cisterns, a post office, warehouses, and wharves. At its prime, the key had 40 to 50 permanent inhabitants. He brought in topsoil and landscaped it with tropical plants.

Housman was ambitious. In an effort to become independent of Key West, he persuaded the legislative council to establish Dade County in 1836, with tiny Indian Key as the county seat. But soon thereafter, he began to decline in personal fortunes. He eventually lost his wrecker's license, and at the outbreak of the Second Seminole War in 1835, he also lost his Indian trade and had to mortgage the island. In stepped Dr. Henry Perrine, a physician with a passion for tropical botany. He moved to the key with great plans to cultivate agave for the manufacture of hemp, but he also wanted to cultivate tea, coffee, bananas, and mangos. He started a nursery on the mainland at Matecumbe.

In 1840, a band of more than 100 Indians attacked the island. Housman and his wife managed to escape, but Dr. Perrine was killed and his house set on fire.

Except for one building and many stone foundations, all of Indian Key was leveled. It was never rebuilt. Housman sold Indian Key and returned to Key West, where he managed to fit back into the establishment he had snubbed.

Since the early 1900s, Indian Key has remained uninhabited. Dr. Perrine's plants—sisal plants, cactus, and wild tamarind among them—are still here in great profusion, as are an observation tower, ruins of a warehouse, a tropical hotel, and a U.S. Navy hospital. There is a boat dock, a shelter, and walking trails, but no rest rooms or picnic facilities. The grave of Jacob Housman is also located here, marked by a plaque.

Indian Key Festival, a weekend historical reenactment, is held each October. For this festival, transportation is provided from Indian Key Fill at MM 78.5. Money raised helps fund the nonprofit group, Friends of Islamorada State Parks, which preserves and protects natural resources while keeping them open to the public.

As is true with all Florida state parks, please be careful while on the island. You may not dig or remove any artifacts nor feed any wild animals. Alcohol and firearms are prohibited, as are pets. Ranger-guided tours are available Thursday through Monday at 9:00 A.M. and 1:00 P.M. only. You board a boat at Robbie's (MM 77.5 bay side) at 8:30 A.M. or 1:30 P.M. Or you can hire a private boat; the island is "open" from 8:00 A.M. to sunset.

*For more information:* Park Ranger, c/o Long Key State Recreation Area, P.O. Box 776, Long Key, FL 33001. Call 305-664-4815, or for Robbie's reservations, call 305-664-9814.


# Anne's Beach

A small ocean-side beach in Islamorada, actually on Lower Matecumbe Key, Anne's Beach is not commercial, which is definitely in its favor. But it is often crowded and parking is at a premium. It has a half-mile elevated, wooden boardwalk which extends through a wetland hammock. Covered picnic areas along the boardwalk and rest rooms at its north end make this a relaxing, quiet place to spend a few hours. Admission is free.

The beach is easy to miss. It's just southwest of Caloosa Cove Resort, or if you're heading north, just past the Channel 2 Bridge at MM 73.5, Lower Matecumbe Key.

*For more information:* Call 305-295-4385.

# Layton Trail

Layton Trail is located at MM 68–69 bay side, just inside Layton, a tiny, incorporated city north of Long Key State Park. A tiny sign marks the trail, but a larger sign proclaims the Long Key Fishing Club, established in 1906 by Flagler's East Coast Hotel Company. The 1935 hurricane destroyed the property. Zane Grey, the Western writer and pioneer of Florida Keys fishing, was once its president. The clear stream that runs from the Atlantic to the boundaries of this small park is named Zane Grey Creek.

The 20-minute walk leads to a rocky shore. Some trees are labeled; you'll see wild coffee, Jamaica dogwood, gumbo limbo, and lots of palms. There is dense overgrowth on this path, and hungry mosquitoes.

# Long Key State Recreation Area

Florida's state parks and recreation facilities advertise themselves as "the Real Florida." These are where you will see a wide variety of species in the wild. All the parks I have visited in the Keys are clean, gorgeous, and peaceful. No high-rise condos or Kmarts are within sight, and you seldom hear a motor of any kind.

Long Key is one of the finest I've visited. Located at MM 67.5 at 67400 Overseas Highway, it offers nature trails, swimming, canoeing, fishing, camping, and educational opportunities such as talks and guided walks. There are plenty of oceanfront picnic tables nestled among towering pine trees. The park is smaller than Bahia Honda, and perhaps a bit less frequented, but I found it equally as appealing.

Long Key opens at 8:00 A.M. and closes at sunset year-round, as do all state parks. There is a small entrance fee and strict rules. Pets are not allowed in camping areas nor on beaches; alcohol, drugs, and ground fires are not permitted; and feeding wild animals is against the law. All state park lands in Florida are managed to appear as they did when the first Europeans came here. Hunting, livestock grazing, and timber removal are not permitted for these reasons.

That said, you'll find a lot to do here. It would be wonderfully relaxing to spend a few days at Long Key with binoculars, a couple of good books, a sketch pad or journal, a camera, and a bathing suit.

If you like walking, there are three trails within the park's limits: a well-labeled boardwalk trail that winds over a thick mangrove-lined lagoon and includes an observation tower; a sandy nature trail that takes one hour to walk; and the Golden Orb Trail, named after the golden orb weaver spider. This passes through a mangrove creek, with a sandy berm above and a narrow beach. On high ground you enter a tropical hammock.

Layton Trail, just inside the Layton town limit, before Long Key State Park, is across the highway from the park. (See previous entry.)

Back in the main park, a one-and-one-quarter-mile winding canoe trail is appropriate for both novice and more experienced boaters, and the waters off the ocean-side beach are swimmable all year, as are all Keys waters.

In spring 1997, Long Key participated in a shoreline restoration project, which will help the native dune plants protect the shoreline from further erosion and create a natural sea turtle nesting area.

On one of the park's brochures, the staff has written: "Thank you for taking only pictures, and leaving nothing but footprints." This is the philosophy of all 141 Florida state parks, which are some of the most pristine and varied in vegetation I have seen anywhere.

*For more information:* Long Key State Recreation Area, P.O. Box 776, Long Key, FL 33001. Call 305-664-4815. Website: http://www.thefloridakeys.com/parks/long.htm.

# San Pedro Underwater Archaeological Preserve

The San Pedro Underwater Archaeological Preserve, one of Florida's oldest artificial reefs, is located within the boundaries of Long Key State Recreation Area. *San Pedro* was a 287-ton ship built in Holland, which sailed in the Spanish fleet of 1733. In 1960, her remains were discovered here in Hawk Channel. Small silver coins dated between 1731 and 1733 were discovered in the salvage attempts, as were parts of rigging and hardware such as keys, and her cargo of Mexican and Chinese ceramics. Although there were numerous salvaging efforts in the 1960s, all that remains of the vessel is a large pile of ballast stones. However, the popular diving site, in a white sand pocket with a variety of marine life, has been jazzed up with seven replica cannons, an anchor, and an educational plaque. Fish such as parrotfish, angelfish, grunts, and at least one barracuda are visible.

This is designated an Underwater Archaeological Preserve. The site is a joint project of the Florida Department of State, Division of Historical Resources, and the Florida Department of Natural Resources, Division of Recreation and Parks. The purpose is to encourage appreciation and understanding of remnants of Florida's maritime heritage. No spearfishing is allowed on-site, and the use of metal detectors is forbidden. Of course, take only pictures, not any living creatures—plants or coral.

*San Pedro* is located in 18 feet of water, approximately one and a quarter nautical miles south of Indian Key. It is important to tie up to mooring buoys located at the site to avoid anchor damage.

**For more information:** Long Key State Recreation Area, P.O. Box 776, Long Key, FL 33001. Call 305-664-4815.

# Islamorada

Islamorada is known as the sportfishing capital of the world. I have not included fishing in this resource book, but there still is plenty to do and see in this sleepy, sunny town. Its name comes from Spanish explorers who sailed by this island, saw the purple hue to its coastline from lavender shells of sea snails, and gave it the name, "*islas moradas,*" which means purple isles. Nearly 4,000 years ago, Calusa Indians lived on this small clump of islands. The purple snails are gone now, too. The total area has approximately 8,287 acres. The Islamorada area extends from MM 86 to MM 66, from Plantation Key to Long Key.

The area is primarily known for its diving, boating, swimming, sunning, and the aforementioned fishing. Of course, if you're of this persuasion, you can catch and release. The original coral formation of these islands can best be seen at Windley Key Fossil Reef State Geological Site, MM 85.

As you will discover, the area hosts a number of historical and archaeological sites: the state parks of Indian Key,

Lignumvitae Key, the San Pedro Underwater Park, and the Theater of the Sea. The Islamorada chamber of commerce is looking at two sites on which to build a new visitor center and museum, and the staff is anxious to please. When the new center is completed, Flagler railroad buildings, a nature trail, and ship's cannon will also be on-site.

For divers and snorkelers, this area is ideal. You'll find lighthouses marking the demise of large ships, shallow depths, mid-range reefs, steep canyons, as well as numerous wrecks. Also here is the *San Pedro* site, now a state park. Several dive boats depart twice daily. Pick up brochures at the chamber of commerce at MM 82.6 in downtown Islamorada. One other thing about this area: the farther north from Key West you travel, the less expensive are lodging and restaurants. Family-style cabins and motels are abundant as are diner-style restaurants and seafood joints.

# 2

# The Middle Keys

## Marathon

In the heart of the Keys, less than one hour north of Key West, the town of Marathon (population approximately 15,000) could be in a different country. It includes the area between MM 65 and MM 40. Sure, it has the same palm trees, the same pelicans and herons as Key West, but the feel is much more rural, even suburban in parts, and much more sporting. Unlike Key West's city feeling, Marathon is woods and an overdeveloped strip. Sportfishing is one of the most popular activities, as is hanging out in several small seafood restaurants or snack bars. Marathon is a good place to bring a family, to stay in a campground or in a housekeeping cabin, to swim, dive, boat, and fish all day long.

The Marathon area stretches between the famous and breathtaking Seven-Mile Bridge on one end and Grassy Key, home of the Dolphin Research Center, at the other. It incorporates Conch Key, Duck Key, Grassy Key, Crawl Key, Fat Deer Key, and the largest, Vaca (Spanish for cow) Key. This was so named for its abundance of manatees (also known as sea cows).

The name *Marathon* supposedly refers to the huge manual task that Henry Flagler's railroad construction crews faced as they built a bridge across a stretch of seven miles of open sea.

The Old Seven-Mile Bridge now takes you (on foot or in a trolley) to Pigeon Key (see Index). This section of bridge was designated a historic monument in 1980.

Opened in 1982, the new bridge, called "the crown jewel of Keys bridges," is where you'll see one of the best views in the whole chain of Keys, perhaps in the country. It's stunning every time you see it. This bridge is made up of 288 135-foot sections, built in Tampa and hauled by barge to the Keys for assembly. It is the longest segmented bridge in the world.

Marathon is also famous for the Kmart, a landmark right smack in the center of town. This is not a joke. Clothing, accessories, and souvenirs are not inexpensive in Key West; they *are* at Kmart, and you can shop to your heart's content for flamingo, palm tree, or shell motifs.

Highlights in Marathon for the nature lover include the Crane Point Hammock and Museum of the Florida Keys, the Florida Keys Children's Museum, historic Pigeon Key, and Sombrero Beach, where you can see the adorable and endangered burrowing owl. Watch for brown pelicans and cormorants on bridges and docks, and osprey nests atop power poles.

If you're in search of a good local book selection, check out the wide variety of both new and used editions at Book Key & Gallery, MM 53 bay side. If you're hungry, try the award-winning Key lime pie at 7-Mile Grille, MM 47 bay side.

While in the Marathon area, enjoy the sun, the surf, and, as the locals add, "the suds."

# The Dolphin Connection at Hawk's Cay Resort and Marina

In the Keys, you'll see many signs leading to dolphin-related businesses. Beware. Some of these are aboveboard in their treatment of the marine mammal and in their rationale for displaying them, and some are not. For that reason, I've only included a handful of attractions featuring these intelligent creatures. The others aren't here for some good reason—they're not recommended by other dolphin trainers, they keep dolphins in captivity for solely financial reasons, etc. One more note about dolphins in the Keys. When you see *dolphin* on a menu the first time, don't despair or call the waiter to complain. This dolphin is quite another species—the dolphin fish, a greenish-blue and yellow fish that grows to 30 pounds.

One of the better places to get close to a real dolphin is at one of the Dolphin Connection's three-times-a-day Dolphin Discovery programs. In this program, you will learn a great deal about the physiology, biology, and habitat of the Atlantic bottlenose dolphin and you will interact with, and even touch, one or two dolphins. You'll also learn a little about whales and porpoises. You will not swim with the dolphin, but you will certainly make a strong connection.

The site's trainer attracts the dolphins using tape recordings of echolocation sounds. Dolphins apparently do like to interact with humans; it doesn't take much to get them performing or participating. Of course, a fish snack always helps. The dolphins put their heads on the feet of participants sitting on a dock in the animals' enclosed pool.

Two dolphins were taking part in this program when I visited. The space they were sequestered in seemed large, and there were many signs on the property about the care and protection of the dolphin and its habitat. The creatures seemed well cared for and admired, and the participants certainly learn a good deal about this intelligent marine mammal.

A sign at the facility reads: "One primary purpose of the Dolphin Connection is to ensure a sustainable dolphin population for the future. Several dolphins have been born here at Hawk's Cay." Another sign relayed the information that the Dolphin Connection, in early 1997, was involved in a research project in which dolphins were observed and compared in the wild in Florida Bay, at Hawk's Cay, and at the Brookfield Zoo's Seven Seas Panorama.

The downside to this program is twofold. Of course, these dolphins are being held in captivity, primarily, it appears, as a tourist attraction. The other is that this program, as intimate a look at the creatures as it provides, is expensive. The rate in January 1997 was $70.00 per person for a 45-minute program. The day I visited, only one very lucky 10- or 11-year-old boy learned about these special creatures up close. Lots of observers, including me, had to stand on the balcony and merely watch the program.

To find the place, look for signs for Hawk's Cay Resort, slightly north of Marathon at MM 61. Drive in and around to the left and enter through the main lobby of the hotel; walk through to the left. Reservations are necessary; shows are at 10:00 A.M., 1:00 P.M., and 4:00 P.M. daily. Alcohol and photography are not allowed.

*For more information:* The Dolphin Connection, Hawk's Cay Resort, 61 Hawk's Cay Boulevard, Duck Key, FL 33050. Call 305-289-9975. Fax 305-289-0136.

# Dolphin Research Center

If you are a fan of "Flipper" TV shows or movies, you'll be interested to know that many generations of Flipper were trained at the Dolphin Research Center (DRC). The first Flipper's real name was Mitzi, and a monument to her memory is installed here. Many dolphins have since played Flipper; the movies were filmed at this location until 1994. The marine educational center's dolphins still star in films, documentaries, calendars, and print ads.

A marine center first opened at this site in 1958 under the name of Santini's Porpoise School. Today's facility was formed in 1984, and its goals then and now were the establishment of a nonprofit (and today publicly funded) educational and research facility. If you only visit one dolphin site, I'd recommend this one.

The DRC now maintains a colony of approximately 19 dolphins and 3 California sea lions in a natural, if confined, environment. They live in 90,000 square feet of saltwater lagoons, an average of 15 feet deep, with low fences separating them from the Gulf of Mexico.

Many of the dolphins were born here. The center believes that birth in a controlled setting reduces the need for collecting dolphins from the wild and provides statistics on intelligence and physical and sexual development. Others have been rescued from traveling road shows and carnivals. Such is the case with Molly, one of the oldest residents at 41, almost double the average age of 20 to 25. An original promise the staff made was that all the dolphins that live there will always have a secure and loving home. That appears to be the case; these creatures look healthy and act lively.

The DRC is also a member of the Southeast Stranding Network, a rescue team which rehabilitates surviving beached whales and dolphins, and is affiliated with the Make-a-Wish Foundation, Dream Factory, and other associations that raise money to fulfill sick children's wishes. More recently, it has extended its rescue commitment to include the endangered manatee and is the only facility in the Florida Keys working with this endangered species. (For more information on the gentle manatee, see the sidebar on page 47.)

The Dolphin Research Center offers one-hour guided walking tours five times a day. (A wheelchair-accessible trail has been recently added.) These are highly informative and entertaining tours on which you learn about the marine mammals' life cycles, echolocation, intelligence, and community life. You also watch dolphins follow commands—jumping, flipping, and frolicking in a joyous, contagious manner. These creatures can leap more than 23 feet in the air, and can swim 20 miles per

*Dolphin*

hour. On every tour I have taken, the tour leaders and trainers seem enthusiastic and genuinely fond of their wards.

If you wish to learn a bit more, a new "Tips on Training" program is available. For one half hour, you can join trainers and dolphins to learn what they do, and you get to touch a dolphin. This is a walk-in, no reservation program, beginning at 1:30 P.M. After you finish the program, you may join the regularly scheduled tour.

Other, longer programs are also offered. For example, you can take what is called DolphInsight, a half-day program offered three times a week in which you learn about the facility and dolphin physiology. This also provides the opportunity to actually touch and communicate with a dolphin by using verbal and hand signals. In 1998, the price was $75.00 per person.

Dolphin Encounter includes a structured, fun swim session with an educational workshop and tour. This workshop is $90.00 per person. A veritable bargain here is that family members of the swimmers may attend the workshops and accompany the tour (but not swim) for $15.00.

The center's week-long program is called Dolphinlab. You can receive academic credits for this experience through Florida Keys Community College, which has branches in both Marathon and Key West. In this intensive program, you learn of ongoing research concerning dolphins, the marine environment, and related issues. You get to know all the dolphins individually, swim with them, prepare their food, and learn a few training techniques. No prior experience is necessary. Minimum age is 18, and the cost is $1,050, which includes room, board, and transportation associated with classes. Intermediate or advanced Dolphinlab programs are available for those who may want to start a career working with dolphins.

Of course, once you swim with or touch these curious, gentle creatures, you're likely to instinctively become more connected to the species and more concerned about its welfare.

The other activity of this facility is its valuable research program, which has apparently been reduced at present. Two previous research projects involved DNA fingerprinting, newly developed genetic techniques to assess the application of molecular techniques to field studies of wild marine animal populations; and metacognition, which investigates the creatures' consciousness. This is important not only as a way of documenting the cognitive abilities of dolphins, but also in suggesting new ways to foster self-awareness and self-control in children with mental disabilities, since swimming with dolphins is incredibly peaceful and stress reducing. Between 1988 and 1994, behavioral therapy techniques were explored using children with Down's syndrome, cerebral palsy, and attention deficit disorder. This project is now on hold, but the research facility plans a long-term followup of the children, and expects to work with more therapists and participants in the near future.

On the premises is an environmental gift shop, the highlights of which are the T-shirts and sweatshirts (called Dolph Art Tees) painted by the resident dolphins. In fact, when I last visited the DRC in January 1996, I watched two dolphins take up paintbrushes and create another wearable abstract masterpiece. The proceeds of these clothing items go to buy the fish that the dolphins and sea lions eat in huge quantities. The gift shop also stocks books, videos, and audiotapes, dolphin screensavers, CD-ROMs, and a myriad of educational games. You can become a member of the Dolphin Society or become an adoptive dolphin parent.

The center is open daily except Christmas, Thanksgiving, and New Year's Day and is located at U.S. Highway 1, MM 59 bay side, at Grassy Key just north of Marathon.

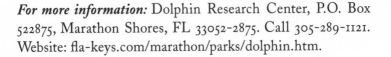

***For more information:*** Dolphin Research Center, P.O. Box 522875, Marathon Shores, FL 33052-2875. Call 305-289-1121. Website: fla-keys.com/marathon/parks/dolphin.htm.

# The Museum of Natural History and the Florida Keys Children's Museum

Two museums in one, opened in 1990, the Museum of Natural History and the Florida Keys Children's Museum are located in the Crane Point Hammock on what was once a pre-Colombian Bahamian village, a 63.36-acre property in Marathon. They are almost exactly opposite the Kmart shopping center. Located at MM 50.5 on the gulf side of the road, the museums, owned and operated by the Florida Keys Land and Sea Trust, a private nonprofit conservation organization, are open daily. In addition, you can meander along walking trails, visit a historic home, and buy souvenirs in a nature-related gift shop.

The visitor center contains many exhibits including a Keys butterfly exhibit, a sea turtle exhibit, and alligator and crocodile information and models. In one corner of the building, you're transported to the ocean floor—fish, turtle, and coral models line this ocean's walls, which are aquamarine and lumpy as underwater reefs or stones might be. A large chart of the fishes of the sea, including information on the living coral reef and how you can help save it, is also displayed.

Also fascinating is a Native American display. Three tribes once lived in the Keys: the Calusa, who disappeared in the 1700s; the Tequestas, who disappeared about the same time; and the Seminoles, many of whom still live throughout the

Everglades and Big Cypress Swamp. You will learn that the Keys are more than 800 islands, most of them uninhabited.

In an adjacent building reached by a bridge is the science activity center for kids, consisting of a local shell exhibit, aquariums, and a children's library of nature books that also offers comfortable chairs and a series of marine touch tanks. The shells displayed here represent the seashore memories of Mrs. Marian Romine, who donated her collection and funded the cabinets in which to display them.

Outside is one of the largest iguanas I have ever seen—a male about nine years old. You also might see a bright-green juvenile iguana running around on the bridge. Many iguanas are abandoned; people don't realize they are not exactly cuddly, affectionate pets when they purchase them. The iguanas at this museum are just such orphans.

Also on the property is an amphitheater used for presentations to school groups on topics ranging from plants to fish to activities of the nearby Dolphin Research Center or Turtle Hospital.

In back of the buildings is a quarter-mile nature trail with interpretive markers. Various palms, gumbo limbo (nicknamed the tourist tree because its bark turns red and peels like a sunburn), and bird habitats are marked. Approximately 160 native and 50 exotic plants can be seen here.

About 10 minutes back along the coral trail is the recently restored Adderley House, built in 1903. This is one of few remaining examples of Black Bahamian architecture known as tabby construction. The house is tiny, with one wooden floor and no windows; Bahama shutters are pulled down to keep out the heat. Its original owner, George Adderley, was a boatman, sponger, turtler, and Episcopal lay preacher who died in Key West in 1958. The building is being restored by the Florida Keys Land & Sea Trust. The museum staff hopes to furnish the house with period pieces in the near future.

For more adventurous hikers, another half-mile trail extends to the Florida Bay, offering open water views and exotic trees around the historic Crane House, which is occupied by the National Marine Sanctuary.

The Crane Point Hammock Museums are open year-round except Christmas day. Guided nature tours are offered once a week; otherwise, the museum's exhibits and trails are self-guided and explanatory. This is an especially good activity for families and should take between one and three hours to complete.

*For more information:* Call 305-743-9100.

# West Indian Manatee

The gentle, giant manatee, an endangered marine mammal, swims in many of Florida's warm waters, and you may well see one while visiting the Keys. I've seen one in Key West waters and others up north, around Key Largo. Known also as sea cows, manatees are gray or gray-brown and so ungainly, they're lovable. These slow-moving creatures are vegetarians, feeding just below the surface on submerged plants. They can grow to 15 feet long, weigh almost a ton, and live as long as 32 years. They are most often seen in the winter. In 1996, the statewide survey counted 2,274. (The total U.S. population was 2,639 that year.)

Christopher Columbus was the first white man to see this aquatic beast, which belongs to the sirenia order, a lineage that includes dugongs and elephants. In the waters of Haiti, the manatee seemed to be half woman, half fish, an unlikely mermaid. *Sirenia* means "the seductive ladies of the sea." Forty-five-million-year-old fossils related to manatees have been discovered in Florida.

Their worst enemy is the speedboat, with propellers that often nick or even kill them. Every adult manatee I've seen has cut marks on his or her back. A law was passed in July 1978 making it mandatory for boaters to reduce their speed in critical habitat areas between November 15 and March 31. Many manatees also die from toxins produced by microorganisms, popularly known as red tide. In August 1997, researchers at the University of Miami also identified the first cases of a virus that caused skin lesions in the manatees. On the plus side, manatees have been protected since 1970 under the Federal Marine Mammal Protection Act and the Endangered Species Act. If you find an injured or dead manatee while in the Keys, please call the Florida Marine Patrol toll free at 800-342-1821 or 800-342-5367.

Outside the Keys, in your Florida travels, you might see wild manatees at these places: Blue Spring State Park, Orange City; Crystal River National Wildlife Refuge, Crystal River; Fanning Springs State Recreation and Conservation Area, Fanning Springs; Marinella Gardens Park, Port Everglades in Fort Lauderdale; Merritt Island National Wildlife Refuge, Merritt Island; Moore's Creek, Fort Pierce; Orange River, Fort Myers; Tampa Electric Company, Apollo Beach; and Wakulla River and the St. Marks River in St. Marks.

**For more information:** Save the Manatee® Club's Emergency Rescue Fund, write Save the Manatee® Club, 500 N. Maitland Avenue, Maitland, FL 32751. Call 800-432-JOIN.

---

# Marathon Garden Club

On the gulf side in Marathon, just north of the prominent Kmart, you'll see a small sign indicating the Marathon Garden Club. Yes, it's open to the public, Tuesday through Saturday, from 10:00 A.M. to 2:00 P.M., and to groups by appointment. The gardens are an original part of a former nursery.

The gardens' specialties include Australian tree ferns, lipstick palms, and orchids. The center holds plant sales twice a year, in November and March or April, and often serves as the site of wedding receptions. There is no charge to tour the gardens but the club asks for donations. Keeping gardens fresh and beautiful (not dry) is an expensive proposition in southern Florida.

*For more information:* Call Char Merritt at 305-743-2064, or the center at 305-743-4971. Merritt is away during the summer months.

# Sombrero Beach

Sombrero, a small, never crowded beach in Marathon, seems to attract mostly local English- and Spanish-speaking families. People often have barbecues or picnics here. There are some picnic tables (several shaded), a small outdoor shower to wash off the salt water, a playground, and a baseball diamond.

Unlike some Key West beaches, this does not feel like the backdrop of a beauty contest. People come here to enjoy the sun, their families, and water that is always bath temperature. This is a good beach for swimming; the water is deep and the sand immaculate.

But for those looking for wildlife at this beach off the beaten path, the primary attraction is the endangered burrowing owl. On the mowed grass next to the beach are three fenced-in enclosures for these small, diurnal birds of prey. Signs posted on the fences say they are federally protected.

A small brown owl originally of the prairies and open grasslands of the West (often living near prairie dog communities), the bird can sometimes be seen sitting on the ground,

even in the midday heat, turning its small head around inquis-
itively or bobbing it up and down. These sandy brown–colored
birds are about eight or nine inches tall and have long legs
and a stubby tail. They do what looks like deep-knee bends
when agitated, but you can't get close enough to see this at
Sombrero Beach. If a young owl is disturbed in its hole, the
bird gives a call that some believe imitates a rattlesnake's
buzzing tail. The owls nest from February to August. (Note:
after Hurricane Georges, I couldn't find the owls; hopefully,
they will return to nest on this beach.)

Other birds commonly seen on this beach are several varieties of gulls and the brightly colored black skimmer.

Fond of open grassy areas, the burrowing owl can also be
seen at the small, municipal Marathon Airport, though infre-
quently. Get permission from the airport manager, however,
before walking around the airport. One year, an owl had a
burrow on the football field of Marathon High School, about
half a mile from the beach.

To reach Sombrero Beach, heading north from Key West,
follow Sombrero Road to the middle of Marathon. Take a
right on Route 1 at the traffic light between the NationsBank
and the Texaco station. Sombrero Beach is two miles ahead
on your left. Parking is plentiful; no entry fee is charged.

# Hidden Harbor Turtle Hospital and SAVE-A-TURTLE

Until quite recently, I had never "known" any sea turtles and
those I had seen, although worthy of praise for their stoic
antiquity (their fossil record dates back 150 million years),
seemed untouchable and uncommunicative. After visiting the
Florida Keys many times, and specifically after visiting Blue

Hole in Big Pine Key, I became curious about and empathetic to these large, hard-shelled reptiles.

Five major types of sea turtles live in the Keys (only seven species are recognized worldwide): loggerhead, which can weigh up to 350 pounds; green, in the 200- to 300-pound range; leatherback, up to one ton; hawksbill, up to 200 pounds; and Kemp's ridley, up to 100 pounds. Only 5,000 Kemp's ridleys are believed to still exist in the wild; they are the rarest sea turtle in the world. All but the loggerhead are endangered in Florida, but that sea turtle is classified as threatened under the federal Endangered Species Act.

Sea turtles have existed for at least 200 million years, when their terrestrial ancestors shared the earth with the dinosaurs. They took to the water and for at least 100 million years, have been adapted to the sea. When dinosaurs became extinct, turtles were able to live on, probably because of their hard shells.

In the Keys is the only known hospital in the world devoted solely to the care of these rare and somber creatures. The Hidden Harbor Turtle Hospital, behind the Hidden Harbor Motel in Marathon, was founded in the mid-1980s by motel owner Richie Moretti and sea captain Tina Brown after they and area fishers found numerous turtles twisted in fishing nets. What was once a human saltwater swimming pool for guests is now a holding pool for turtles. The licensed, non-profit operation is run entirely by volunteers; proceeds from the motel fund the animals' care, food, and necessary surgical and other medical equipment. Funds are also used toward much-needed research. Donations are always helpful.

This is *not* a tourist attraction. Only people rescuing turtles (the hospital has a turtle ambulance) or motel guests are allowed on the premises to watch the feeding or the occasional surgery. There are surgical facilities, several ponds, and large containers for individual turtles. Turtles receive shots and special diets, may have ivs, and may require surgery. Local vets donate their time. It takes several people to lift many of these creatures. The turtle hospital works closely with the University of Florida at Gainesville, which is involved in an ongoing research project on intestinal viruses and fibropapilloma. For several years, the Florida green sea turtles have been developing fibropapilloma, tumorlike growths on soft body tissue, shells, and around the eyes. Over 50 percent of the green sea turtles in the waters off the Keys may have some form of this cancer, and it has begun to affect the Loggerhead population, too.

When I visited the turtle hospital, 63 loggerheads and greens were in residence. Also on-site were two abandoned iguanas, watching over the scene with great interest. Volunteer Jeanette Hobbs told me that some sea turtles live there permanently because boat injuries cause them to float, rather than be able to get to the bottom and feed. One resident was blind. All sea turtles infected with fibropapilloma develop tumors on their eyes, but if one eye retains good vision, the creature can be released.

The turtles are fed red herring, shrimp, and squid. Baby turtles are fed Purina Turtle Chow. In the tanks large tarpon and jewfish swim with the adult turtles. The tarpon keep the reptiles more active because they provide competition for the food.

One recent fairly typical resident was Mono, a turtle found with monofilament around one front flipper and her neck. Her flipper had to be amputated, and some of the ligaments and tendons in her neck had to be cut. After a few months in a special rehabilitation pond, Mono became healthy enough to be released back into the ocean.

All turtles are tagged when they leave this hospital; no news of them is considered good news. Not all the quiet creatures can be released, of course, and Moretti has promised them a home until their natural deaths. This is quite a promise, considering their possible life span of 100 years.

The Turtle Hospital has won several awards for its kind care. One of the most recent was in December 1997 when it received a conservation and preservation award from the Society of American Travel Writers. The Marathon-based hospital continues to lead research efforts, along with the University of Florida, to combat a herpes-type virus that results in growth of tumors on turtles around the world.

Numerous factors have contributed to the sea turtles' dramatic decline in Florida. Of course, for a long time turtles meant steaks, soups, and chowders. In many parts of the world, their meat, shells, and even flipper leather are still in great demand. Nowadays, beach-cleaning equipment, dune buggies, and other vehicles can destroy unhatched nests; trash can entrap hatchlings and adults. Out in the ocean, turtles may become entangled in fishing line, be hit by boats, or drown in commercial shrimpers' nets.

Sea turtles have not had a happy history in the Keys. For many years, green turtles weighing up to 500 pounds were netted in the ocean as far away as Nicaragua. After they were hoisted up onto the schooner's deck, the turtles were laid on their backs with their flippers tied and periodically splashed with salt water. This was done to keep the turtles alive. Hawkbills were harpooned when they surfaced to breathe. The harpoon pierced just below the shell so as not to kill the animals. The creatures were then brought into Key West where they were held in tidal-flushed corrals at the Turtle Kraals (now a popular restaurant which, until fairly recently, also housed the Wildlife Rescue of the Florida Keys) and butchered as needed. The turtle meat was cut into steaks, ground into burgers, or used in chowder. The belly, shell, and flippers were used in soup, first canned in 1895. Fortunately, in 1973, the Endangered Species Act made it illegal to "harass, harm, pursue, hunt, shoot, wound, kill, capture, or collect endangered species." All sea turtles are protected under both federal and state laws and may not be possessed, harassed, or disturbed in any way.

If you come across a stranded or injured sea turtle while visiting the Keys, call the Turtle Hospital at 305-743-6509. You should also report the injured animal to the Florida Marine Patrol at 800-Dial-FMP.

An organization that is related to the hospital is SAVE-A-TURTLE, a volunteer nonprofit group founded in 1985 and sponsored by the Florida Park Service, the Game and Fresh Water Fish Commission, and St. James the Fisherman Church. Its purpose is to help preserve and protect sea turtles and provide related education. It does the latter for both schoolchildren and the general public, and produces a monthly newsletter, *Turtle Tracks*. Each year, between April and September, trained and authorized volunteers patrol local beaches for turtle nests and protect them when necessary. Turtles can lay up to 120 eggs, but many never hatch.

The good news in early 1998: in the Keys, excluding the Dry Tortugas, total turtle hatchlings increased from 4,856 in 1996 to 8,934 in 1997; total nests increased from 110 in 1996 to 128 in 1997, however, 5,269 did not hatch compared to 5,119 the year before. Still, it's progress.

You may also adopt a baby turtle. Adopting a single turtle costs $10.00, twins $20.00. For each one adopted, you receive an individual certificate and a photo of your baby turtle, and you can give it the name of your choice. The funds will help all sea turtles in the Keys.

Here are a few suggestions on how to help protect and save sea turtles in the Florida Keys:

- Never disturb or harass nesting turtles. According to Jeanette Hobbs, the later in the season the babies hatch, the smaller chance they have of surviving.
- Watch out for hatchlings that become disoriented by headlights and lured onto the road. May 1 to October 31 is the hatching season.
- When you are boating, avoid collisions with turtles.
- Don't throw trash in the water, and pick up all litter from the beach.
- Never buy products (like soup or tortoiseshell jewelry or accessories) made from sea turtles. It is illegal to bring these products into the United States.
- Purchase a sea turtle sticker or poster from the Florida Department of Natural Resources. All proceeds support the state's sea turtle recovery program.

***For more information:*** Hidden Harbor Turtle Hospital, 2396 Overseas Highway, Marathon, FL 33050. Call 305-743-6509. Fax 305-743-2552.

SAVE-A-TURTLE, P.O. Box 361, Islamorada, FL 33036. Call 305-743-6056.

# Pigeon Key

Pigeon Key is often called the most photographed spot in the Florida Keys because of its graceful ambiance and spectacular beauty. With its waving palms, wooden camplike buildings, and lack of commercialism, it makes you feel as though you have stepped back in time. This is certainly the way the Keys must have looked originally—or at least the way we hope they looked.

Pigeon Key is a five-acre island two and two-tenths miles due west of Marathon, just off Route 1, at MM 48; it can be reached on foot or by trolley. The Pigeon Key Foundation leased the island from Monroe County in 1993 and began restoring the village. A historic district on the National Register of Historic Places, Pigeon Key served as a construction and maintenance camp for Flagler's railroad, specifically the Old Seven-Mile Bridge portion, from 1908 to 1912. Four hundred workers lived on the island in dormitory-style buildings and tents. When the Old Seven-Mile Bridge was completed, a village was established on the island to house bridge tenders and maintenance workers.

Since 1935, Pigeon Key has served as a center for the Road and Toll District (when the road was a toll road in the 1930s), a base for the U.S. Navy, and a fishing camp. It is currently used as a part-time research center for the University of Miami. At one time, there were also a school and dairy cows here.

Seven charming wooden buildings from the early 20th century remain. One is the Negro Quarters (also called the VIP House), built around 1912 and listed on the Black History Register; it is on the east side of the island. The structure housed mostly black workers, predominantly cooks. This serves as dormitory space for Pigeon Key education programs, and is being restored.

The Old Section Gang's Quarters, built around 1912, was also a dormitory for railway workers and later a mess hall. It then became a restaurant and a lab for the University of Miami. The darkest part of its flooring is original Dade County pine. The structure is now the community building and education center, and was the first building to be restored. Here, you will start your self-guided tour or join a tour led by a volunteer on the staff. Videos and slide presentations are shown regularly.

As far as nature goes, this is an excellent place to just stare down into the water and look at the fish and other marine life on the hard bottom and grass bed. You might see tarpon and sharks, including the hammerhead. The palm trees are especially tall and majestic. Pelicans and cormorants often accompany your walk along the Old Seven-Mile Bridge. On the property is a small white building housing the wet lab for the Mote Marine Laboratory, which conducts marine research here. Experiments in culturing live coral and potential use of coral in bone transplants are being conducted here. Do not enter unless a staff person is present.

The foundation sponsors many residential and day environmental programs for the general public and for school-children on Pigeon Key. Among them are programs on coastal habitats, coral reefs, marine mammals, sea turtles, protected areas, and water quality.

The only way to get to Pigeon Key is to park and walk (or bike or skate) over the Old Seven-Mile Bridge or to take a historic railroad-car shuttle, which runs between 10:00 A.M. and 4:00 P.M. Cars are no longer used on the bridge or on the island.

I've walked the bridge a few times. It's a long and gorgeous walk, a bit more than two miles in full sun. Wear comfortable shoes, wear sunscreen, and carry a water bottle. You'll find no shade until you reach Pigeon Key.

For this excursion, you will want to bring a camera and binoculars, a sketch pad, journal, or book, and a picnic lunch. You can't buy anything to eat or drink here, but you may well want to spend a large part of a day. It is a quiet and peaceful place, never full of people. It's a place you will be inspired to write about, to photograph, to dream about.

Admission is $2.00 per person to walk around the island. All donations are tax deductible. Tours are held daily except on Monday. The visitor center and a quality gift shop are in a railroad car remaining from the Florida East Coast Railway, on the right of Route 1 heading north, on Knight Key.

*For more information:* Pigeon Key Foundation, P.O. Box 500130, Marathon, FL 33050. Call 305-289-0025.

## Veteran's Memorial Park

Veteran's Memorial Park is a tiny, uncrowded, pretty beach at MM 40, on Little Duck Key. It is located at the southern end of the new Seven-Mile Bridge. Bring a book and a chair and stay awhile. Although it does have picnic tables and rest rooms, you may not camp or launch a boat here. Pets are allowed.

---

# Travelers Tree

Although it looks deceptively palmlike, the travelers tree is not truly a palm, but rather a member of the banana family, originally from Madagascar. Outstanding in appearance, it consists of a palmlike trunk supporting a broad fan-shaped top made from eight to a dozen long banana-tree-like leaves. These leaves may be 10 feet long and 2 feet wide, and they have a heavy, arching midrib. Because the wind can fray them, they sometimes look slightly disheveled. Small white flowers are encased in canoe-shaped pods attached to a single stalk, although I've never seen these. The whole plant resembles a gigantic, partially opened, feathery fan.

What's fascinating about these striking tall plants is how they got their name. The fronds are considered to point north and south naturally, thus furnishing the traveler with direction. Because up to a quart of rainwater is stored in the bases of the leaves' heavy, thick stalks, they can provide an unexpected place from which the hot, weary traveler can take a drink. Whether or not people actually drink out of these huge leaves, it makes a romantic story. You'll find travelers trees throughout the Keys; several striking examples can be found on many of Key West's streets.

# Bahia Honda State Park

In Spanish, *bahia honda* means "deep bay." It is also the name of a state park. In 1996, this gorgeous and serene park, located on both the ocean and bay sides of Route 1 at MM 37, was voted the best campsite in Florida by the readers of *Florida Living Magazine*. Once part of the East Coast Railway, its main white, sandy beach was recently selected as the best beach in America by the University of Maryland. Since 1961, the park has been universally considered one of the most spectacular recreation spots in the Keys.

The island of Bahia Honda has long sandy beaches and deep waters close to shore that provide great swimming and snorkeling. The park is made up of 524 acres, including one small island offshore on the southwest end. The geological formation of Bahia Honda is Key Largo limestone, which comes from a prehistoric coral reef similar to today's living reefs in the Keys. Portions of this ancient reef emerged and formed islands or keys, including Bahia Honda.

Many of the plants are unusual, including yellow satinwood, gumbo limbo, the endangered silver palm, and the rare blue Bahia Honda morning glory. You will also find sea oats, one of few plants that can live on sand dunes. Among the birds you might see are the green heron, red-breasted merganser, osprey, American kestrel, five varieties of plovers, nine varieties of gulls and terns, and indigo bunting. You might spot one of several mammals—a raccoon, an evening bat, a rare manatee, or a sleek bottlenose dolphin. Sea turtles, lizards, snakes, and frogs round off the species that are often visible to seasoned and patient eyes.

So what can you do at Bahia Honda State Park? One January weekday, we attended a lively lecture given by two park rangers on the shells and marine life you might encounter while there. A display of shells and sea beans was set on a table.

Sea beans, we learned, are any of a variety of seeds and fruits that are stranded on beaches. These beans may drift for many months and end up on beaches as far away as Greenland or Iceland—any place that comes in contact with the Gulf Stream. One particularly fascinating species was the coin plant, which apparently has been used for jewelry, snuff boxes, aphrodisiacs, and to ward off the "evil eye." The rangers also described fire and soft corals, sea urchins, sea fans, various sponges, stone crabs, and spiny lobsters, also known as crawfish. These lobsters spawn in the mangroves and heavy grass areas. Lobstering is still a significant industry in the Keys. Beginning in early August, the commercial season lasts for six and a half months. Environmentalists are trying to cut the number of licenses awarded by 50 percent in the next five years.

We were also shown various conchs, including the horse conch (the largest), the helmet conch, queen conch, and milk conch. All conchs are protected at this park. A research-replenishment program in the Keys is beginning to raise conchs commercially; they are fed Purina Monkey Chow. In the Keys, all the conch you eat in the form of chowders and fritters comes from the Caribbean.

Along with these daytime lectures (held Monday, Wednesday, and Friday at 11:00 A.M. during the winter season), slide shows on marine-related topics, are held for campers two to three nights a week at 8:00 P.M.

At Bahia Honda State Park you can camp with your own rig or tent in one of 80 sites, or rent one of three duplex cabins. You can eat in the snack bar or buy souvenirs or books and magazines in the gift shop. The two white sand beaches are tranquil and quiet. You can take the Silver Palm Nature Trail, a self-guided walking tour, which brings you to a mangrove, over a dune, and onto the beach. There are a dive shop, snorkeling tours, parasailing opportunities, and boat rentals. You can even rent kayaks and fishing rods. A deposit is required on all rentals, which are reasonably priced. If you have your own boat, the park's marina offers 19 slips, hot showers, and a protected basin. Daytrippers can, of course, use the park for part of a day or an entire day.

The state park system in Florida is well regulated, and generally the parks are pristine. At Bahia Honda, as with all the parks, several rules apply. The park rangers advise visitors never to anchor over coral and to always obtain a navigation chart before exploring the open water. Pets are not allowed, nor is collecting live shells. No alcohol is permitted in any state park. Fourteen days is the maximum length of stay allowed at Bahia Honda. You may set no ground fires, and please do not feed the wild animals.

Florida's 145 state parks are open every day of the year from 8:00 A.M. until sundown. Bahia Honda is an exceptionally peaceful and beautiful place to spend a day or a week.

***For more information:*** Bahia Honda State Park, 36850 Overseas Highway, Big Pine Key, FL 33043. Call 305-872-3210 for concession, tour, and rental information. Call 305-872-2353 for camping, cabin, and park information. Website: http://www .thefloridakeys.com/parks/bahia.htm.

# 3

# The Lower Keys

## Big Pine Key

Big Pine Key is known primarily as the home of the endangered Key deer, but there is a small community here as well. It's the first real town north of Key West, about midway between there and Marathon. You can dive or snorkel here; eat in a number of relatively inexpensive cafes, Cuban restaurants, or seafood restaurants; walk the trails of the Key Deer Refuge; or look at alligators at Blue Hole. Bahia Honda State Park is just a few minutes away. Aside from this, small shopping centers are just off Key Deer Boulevard, in the middle of town, and you'll find a vegetarian cafe and store, as well as one or two good thrift shops (for those of you who, like me, love them).

## Torchwood Hammock Preserve

Torchwood Hammock Preserve, located on Little Torch Key, near Big Pine Key, is considered an ecological jewel by those in the know. Somewhat of a secret, it is home to many rare and endangered species.

The preserve consists of six separate natural communities. The first is a 40-acre rockland hammock. Plants are identified along the trail; more than 60 species of trees and shrubs exist in this portion of the preserve. Creatures you might see are tree frogs, box turtles, raccoons, and the occasional Key deer. Warblers and vireos are common visitors.

The next community you will come to is a coastal-rock barren; the tree canopy is more open than that of the hammock. The ground cover is primarily grasses. Buttonwood trees are predominant in this area, and you'll also see sea daisies, false foxgloves, saffron plums, and many more species.

The third community is the several mosquito ditches, originally built to help control the large mosquito population and colonized by red mangroves. The ditches allow salt water to come into the area and channel and drain standing waste.

Along the shoreline of the preserve is the fourth community—a mangrove fringe natural community, consisting of the red mangrove, the tallest; the black mangrove, the most salt-tolerant; and the white mangrove, the smallest. This area provides shelter for birds such as cormorants, pelicans, ibis, and herons. To see the mangroves, you will need to reach them by way of a kayak or canoe.

Along the southwestern shore of the preserve is the fifth community, a coastal berm, up to 30 feet across in some areas and about 3 feet above sea level. Here you will see a canopy of 15 feet or so, including black torch, blolly, darling plum, and many other species. You will likely encounter land hermit crabs, comical and clumsy yet agile creatures.

The final community is the tidal wetlands, on the preserve north of the east/west extension of Kings Cove Road, which is north of U.S. 1. Found here are salt marshes and scrub mangroves as well as many live birds, fish, crabs, and marine invertebrates. You may see tracks made by various animals too.

Four small fresh-to-brackish ponds are found in the northern half of the wetlands, but they are inaccessible by the trail. The two central ponds provide habitat for the striped mud turtle.

The Torchwood Hammock Preserve is owned and managed by the Florida chapter of the Nature Conservancy, which purchased the 244-acre parcel of land between 1989 and 1991.

This is a fragile area, so the Nature Conservancy asks that you enjoy photography, bird-watching, hiking, canoeing, and other quiet, gentle activities. The following activities are prohibited: bicycling; horseback riding; operating any unauthorized motorized vehicles; removing, disturbing, or introducing any plant, animal, or mineral material; making fires; hunting or fishing; camping; bringing in pets. Please pick up any trash you might find and report any other damage to the Nature Conservancy.

The preserve is on Little Torch Key, approximately 26 miles east of Key West, 2 miles west of Big Pine Key. The entrance to Torchwood is at the southern end of Pirates Road next to the Jolly Roger Estates housing subdivision.

*For more information:* The Nature Conservancy, P.O. Box 4958, Key West, FL 33041. Call 305-296-3880.

# Great White Heron National Wildlife Refuge

Great White Heron is one of four national wildlife refuges in the Florida Keys (all managed by the staff at the Key Deer Refuge on Big Pine), three of which are accessible to the public. Great White Heron Refuge, extending over 264 square miles of open water in the Gulf of Mexico, north of Key West, is reachable only by boat. The U.S. Department of the Interior's Fish and Wildlife Service is in charge of protecting this refuge, created in 1938 to serve as "a refuge and breeding ground for great white herons [the white phase of the great blue heron], other migratory birds and other wildlife." The great white heron, the largest of North America's wading birds, is found only in the Florida Keys and in the southern part of the mainland. The refuge is committed to conservation of fish or wildlife listed as endangered or threatened species under the Endangered Species Act of 1973.

The refuge consists of many small islands, mostly dominated by low mangroves, where flocks of mergansers, terns, wading birds, bald eagles, and osprey roost, nest, and just hang out. Rare birds, like the white-crowned pigeon, roseate spoonbill, and the only known colony of laughing gulls in the lower Keys nest here, too. Endangered or threatened sea turtles use some of these beaches for nesting.

During the early part of this century, great white herons and other sea birds with spectacular plumage dramatically declined in numbers because their long feathers were fashionable in women's hats. Marjory Stoneman Douglas, most famous for her definitive volume, *River of Grass: The Everglades*, also wrote a splendid short story, "Plumes," about the way egrets were treated at this time. After her character, hunter John Pinder, has killed an egret, he thinks, "How much were they paying for plumes? That, too, was unimportant. He had seen them for a little while, glistening in the sun." In 1998 Douglas died at the grand old age of 108.

The islands that make up Great White Heron Refuge are primarily accessible by commercial boats. Strict rules apply on all refuges: no camping, hiking only on designated trails, no fires; no weapons unless cased and left in boats, no metal detectors or removal of artifacts, boats or seaplanes only in designated areas, no feeding or molesting of wildlife or disturbing or removing plants, no storing of equipment. Refuge hours are from a half hour before sunrise to a half hour after sunset. The best seasons to visit are spring, fall, and winter. Summer months are extremely humid, and the mosquitoes sometimes make any water-related wildlife trip much less pleasant.

Organized groups visiting this refuge, or the other two, need to make reservations at refuge headquarters at least two weeks ahead of time.

*For more information:* Call 305-872-2239, or visit the Key Deer Refuge headquarters located in the shopping center off Key Deer Boulevard just north of the traffic light on U.S. 1, on Big Pine Key.

# Skinks and Anoles

When you begin looking closely at tree trunks in the Keys, one of the most startling—and frequent—sights will be a small, rapid reptile with a red throat flap that throbs regularly. (Wouldn't you know? This is the male of the species.) These anoles can be found on most town and city streets throughout South Florida. The brown anole, accidentally introduced from Cuba, can often be seen hunting for insects and spiders, displaying its throat, and courting on the ground. Once you begin to watch for these lizards, you'll see them almost everywhere. They are active during the warmest days, and they burrow occasionally.

Skinks are most common in hammocks. True skinks have a smooth but scaly skin and look a bit like small snakes because their legs are dwarfed and they appear to have no neck. The most common is perhaps the ground skink, three to five inches long. The largest is the broadhead; it can grow to a foot long. The male of this species has a wide head, which turns rusty red in color during the breeding season.

# The Blue Hole

The Blue Hole, an artificial pool, used to be blue, like the natural sinkholes of the Caribbean. It also used to be one of my favorite places to stop in Big Pine Key, either before or after a walk along the nature trails of the National Key Deer Refuge. This was when "Grandpa" lived here, but unfortunately, only his bones are here now, buried somewhere in an unmarked grave. Grandpa was the first gator I cared about. An almost 70-year-old alligator, he was a huge fellow at 10 feet long and approximately 500 pounds. He was moved north to Homasassa Springs in 1993 when some suspected he had grown too fond of forbidden meat and may have caused the demise of a Rottweiler, at the least. Grandpa, who as a youngster had lost an eye to a shooting, died up north, I suspect of a broken heart at being moved away from his natural home. Ironically, he died on my birthday, November 11, in 1994. But he always had his fans, who formed a Save Grandpa Club and moved his remains back to his rightful home.

But, of course, there are still alligators at the Blue Hole. You will enjoy watching them, though few are as large as Grandpa. Alligators, as opposed to crocodiles, thrive in fresh water, though they occasionally swim in brackish or salt water in the Keys. Their snouts are broader and darker than those of their saltwater cousin, the crocodile. They can grow as long as 17 to 19 feet and can live a long, long time.

The breeding season usually begins in late March or April and lasts for about six to eight weeks. Nesting occurs in late May through June on high ground, as the eggs can't survive flooding for more than 12 hours. Between 45 and 60 white, leathery-shelled eggs will be laid in an elaborate nest. Raccoons and snakes can be nest predators. Each mound-type nest is about three inches in diameter. The incubation period is 9 to 10 weeks; hatching occurs around mid-August. At the end of an incubation period, the hatchlings begin to make a sound like a high-pitched grunt within their shells; the high-pitched sound can often be heard 50 feet away. This is a signal for the mother to deconstruct the nest. When born, the babies are about six to eight inches in length and weigh only one or one and a half ounces. Although there is a high survival rate during the first year, after that formative year, the rate drops to only 10 percent.

Archie Carr, a naturalist, writer, and conservationist who spent almost his entire life in Florida, admired alligators. In *A Naturalist in Florida—A Celebration of Eden*, he writes, "The song of the alligator is a vast, rumbling growl that rolls up through the mist of warm dawns like something half sound and half shaking of the earth. One alligator singing alone is a moving thing to hear. Three bellowing in chorus seem to take over the world, to be doing too great a singing for any pond to hold and stay the same."

There are generally at least three gators at the Blue Hole, but there may be more. They live on Big Pine Key and swim with several small turtles, and live at the Blue Hole and in other freshwater ponds; they migrate from hole to hole over land. They will eat almost anything that swims, walks, crawls, or flies—including turtles, fish, Key deer, dogs, and small children. The refuge staff do not feed the gators and neither should you. Feeding introduces foods that might be bad for their diet and teaches them to associate humans with food, increasing their aggressiveness toward humans.

Because some of the big alligators become aggressive in defending their territory, some of the trails are closed. It's important that you observe the warnings and posted signs. If you find a gator out of water, remain at a reasonable distance. Remember that alligators are especially fond of dogs and small children. You won't always see a gator here, but the chances are good that if you're patient and bring along your binoculars, you will.

As Archie Carr writes, "The alligator is just too old for us to lose. He is older than the land he lives in . . . the alligator is a relic of immeasurable value, a world treasure in our charge."

To reach Blue Hole at Big Pine Key, take Route 1 north from Key West. At the traffic lights, take a left onto Key Deer Boulevard; Blue Hole will be on your left just before you arrive at the Key Deer nature trails. It is posted with a small plaque.

# National Key Deer Refuge

National Key Deer Refuge is my favorite natural place in the entire Florida Keys. This national refuge was established in 1957 and is managed by U.S. Fish and Wildlife Service. It is home to the diminutive, endangered species, the Key deer. The deer population, which numbered fewer than 50 in the 1940s, was fairly stable at between 250 and 300 animals for a number of years. However, a surprising new count in late 1998 indicates there now may be as many as 600. Hunting was prohibited by the Florida legislature around 1939.

I have always been drawn to deer—probably prompted by reading Florida resident Marjorie Kinnan Rawlings' *The Yearling* and watching the movie *Bambi* and reinforced during my formative years at our Vermont summer cottage, where each night we watched fawns and their mothers graze.

The first time I visited the Keys, this was one of the first places I wanted to see. I was not disappointed. The small white-tailed Key deer, which only lives in the southernmost tip of Florida, is curious, too friendly for its own good, and stunningly beautiful. I never cease to be thrilled by the dark brown, intelligent eyes, the velvety antlers on the bucks, the reddish-brown color of their hides. I love their black noses, especially in the light of the setting sun. They often stretch their long, sinewy necks up into trees to eat leaves and fruits. As is true with most wild species, the best time to see the Key deer is early in the morning and in the late afternoon or early evening.

The Key deer is a subspecies of the Virginia white-tailed deer. They inhabit and swim between Big Pine Key and 16 surrounding keys. Two-thirds of the population is located on Big Pine Key; cautionary road signs are posted throughout their habitat. The speed limit is 30 MPH throughout the refuge. The area even has a Key deer radio station, 5.30 AM on the dial, which announces the numbers of deer killed in that year. One hundred twenty-five deer were killed in 1997; the number one killer is cars.

The shoulder height of Key deer is between 24 and 28 inches; a doe weighs 45 to 65 pounds, a buck, 55 to 75. They are about the size of German shepherds, but appear much more fragile and graceful. Fawns are born April through June; at birth, the fawns weigh between two and four pounds. The bucks drop their antlers between February and March; their regrowth begins almost immediately. Many deer live eight or nine years.

These deer thrive on native plants including red mangrove, thatch palm berries, and several other species. Fresh water is essential for their survival, although they can tolerate small amounts of salt water, too.

Federal law prohibits disturbing and feeding Key deer and other endangered or threatened species in a National Wildlife Refuge. State regulations also make feeding Key deer a misdemeanor offense. The mammals have already become far too accustomed to living in close proximity to people and to having tourists snap their photos. Too often, they are killed by speeding cars and trucks, or dogs running off their leads. Loss of habitat is also a leading factor in the decline of their numbers.

To get to the refuge, located on Key Deer Boulevard, take a right as you go south on Route 1 in Big Pine Key. About two miles north of the intersection is the refuge trail. The trail is two-thirds of a mile long and posted with markers about its history and a few of the plant species; it winds through pine and palm habitats. At one point, the trail runs adjacent to Watson Hammock, a hardwood area.

But you will also see Key deer along the sides of the small streets that run perpendicular to Key Deer Boulevard and on No Name Key. To get to this small key, take a right on Watson Boulevard off Key Deer Boulevard. Watch for signs for this small, sparsely populated key. (A good bar and restaurant here is the No Name Pub on North Watson Boulevard. It's a hole in the wall nestled among the trees, but it is justly famous for its pizza. The Pub's telephone number is 305-872-9115.) Overnight camping at the refuge or at the nearby Blue Hole is prohibited.

**For more information:** The Refuge Manager, P.O. Box 510, Big Pine Key, FL 33043. Call 305-872-2239. Fax 305-872-3675.

# Hardwood Hammocks

Yes, you may see people taking a siesta in a hammock at midday here in the Keys, but that is not the type of hammock referred to throughout this book. The tropical hardwood hammock is an ecological term that refers to a slightly elevated tract in a swampy area, often densely covered with hardwood trees. Geologists date these tracts as far back as 120,000 years. Hardwood hammocks used to exist as far north as Cape Canaveral, but most northern hammocks have been destroyed. As more and more land is cleared and developed, like many natural wonders, these self-maintaining forest communities are becoming rare. Luckily, they usually remain untouched by fire or flood.

A hardwood hammock is actually an entire forest community, which includes hundreds of species of trees, shrubs, vines, and animals, several of them protected in the Keys. A low canopy of trees covers a wide tangle of shrubs and vines. The hammock sits on limestone and includes trees like gumbo limbo and royal palm in the center, the strangler fig on the next layer out, and red mangroves on the outside. Ground cover is generally sparse because of the limited light that reaches the forest floor. Sometimes the hammock also contains wild bamboo, native to this area. At the edges of a hammock the vegetation is thick with sun-loving trees like Geiger, saffron plum, and wild cotton. Many of these plants have flowers that attract flying insects. These plant and animal communities are quiet, shady, humid, and buggy.

Among the hardwood hammocks you will see are the hammock at the Florida Keys Wild Bird Center in Tavernier, one at the National Key Deer Refuge on Big Pine Key, and one in North Key Largo. A few of the creatures and birds you might encounter are white-crowned pigeons (abundant May through September), warblers, several butterflies (including the giant swallowtail), Key deer, tiny liguus tree snails (for those with good eyes), and perhaps some native lizards. In Key Largo's hammocks live nearly 200 species, including three endangered species: Key Largo wood rat, Key Largo cotton mouse, and Schaus swallowtail butterfly.

According to a report published by the Florida Game and Fresh Water Fish Commission, over 6,000 acres of sensitive hardwood hammock habitat and its related animal species have been preserved in the Florida Keys.

In these fragile Keys, hardwood hammocks are a critical link between upland and sea; they provide stopover points for migratory birds, habitat for many seasonal birds, a home for amphibians and reptiles, and much more.

---

# Perky Bat Tower

You probably won't see any bats on Sugarloaf Key, but the strange, imposing Perky Bat Tower is well worth a short visit. Perky's settlement dates from around 1910, when C. W. Chase started a sponge farm here. During World War I, he sold out to Richter Clyde Perky, who by 1928 was the largest landowner in the chain of Keys. Perky decided to build a luxurious fishing retreat in this rural spot, 17 miles northeast of Key West. The ambitious Perky established a restaurant, gambling casino, marina, and guest cottages. But the overpowering nocturnal mosquitoes drove guests away. So, in 1929, he constructed the bat tower, which cost approximately $10,000. Perched on four wooden posts, the tower was built to lure hungry bats that would clear the area of its prodigious mosquitoes during the wet summer and early fall. Perky's intention was also to house enough bats to produce rich fertilizer for the Keys. As a lure, he imported guano (bat droppings) from Texas.

As luck would have it, no bat ever entered the tower. In fact, two months after it was erected, a storm washed away the bait and deodorized the structure. Perky went bankrupt, his fishing camp burned, and he died. But the bat tower remained. Empty. Today mosquitoes are primarily controlled by sprays dispensed from low-flying airplanes.

The tower itself, made of fading, unpainted cypress shingles that resemble the exteriors of houses on Cape Cod, is about 35 feet tall, built on stilts as are many modern homes in the Keys. It's an oddity worth viewing and maybe photographing.

If you are a bat fan, you might see examples of the Cuban house bat or even the extremely rare Jamaican-Antillean fruit bat in the night sky. The former is relatively new to the Keys, and has been found roosting in old military barracks and under bridges. Colonies have been seen in Marathon, Stock Island, and Boca Chica.

There is no road sign for the bat tower. To get there, take a dirt road to your left as you're heading north, around MM 17 on lower Sugarloaf Key. The road is just to the right of the road that leads to the Sugarloaf Airport, where you will often see people hang gliding or taking sightseeing airplane rides.

As you drive down the dirt road to the isolated wooden tower, keep your eyes open for raccoons and turkey vultures on your right. Red-bellied woodpeckers, wishbone cactus, and date palms are also commonly found on Sugarloaf Key.

***For more information:*** Bat Conservation International, P.O. Box 162603, Austin, TX 78716. The organization produces an attractive, informative, internationally distributed magazine, *Bats*.

# 4

# Key West

## The Southernmost Town in the U.S.

Visiting Key West, population 25,000, is like stepping into an old picture-postcard of Florida. Everything except the bright pink flamingos is here: the pastel cottages, the waving palms, the long, sandy beaches, and the red, languid sunsets. The pace is exceedingly slow. This is the southernmost town in the country, and at the southernmost point, on the ocean side, is a buoy marking just that fact. (This is an extremely popular photo opportunity.)

Key West—made up of locals, Cubans, and transplants from around the world—is a harmonious island, where people feel free to express themselves—through their clothing, haircuts, lifestyles, and bodies, i.e., tattoos and piercings. (A recent "Citizen of the Day" in the daily newspaper said, "If you don't want to be yourself here, be someone else.") It's a literary, artistic, theatrical town. The restaurants are huge in number and almost all of them are excellent.

It's one of the best walking towns I've ever had the joy to discover. Stay off busy Duval Street as much as possible, and venture into the side streets and short, dead-end alleys. Smell the flowers; listen to and admire the wild parrots and the feral roosters. Pet a cat or two. Go to the sunset celebration at Mallory Square once (see Mallory Square entry on page 90).

Although the city has a sophisticated, cosmopolitan feel, there's plenty to do in Key West for nature lovers and protectors. Fort Zachary Taylor Park has an excellent beach; the aquarium is a good place to gain basic information on sea life; Wildlife Rescue of the Florida Keys is doing some of the best environmental work in the Keys, as is Reef Relief. Beaches, parks, historic sites, and environmental organizations are waiting just for you.

# Getting Around Key West

Certainly the best way to get around the city is by foot. You can walk almost everywhere, although walking to the airport from Old Town is a bit of a hike—certainly under five miles, though. If you're not much of a walker, two economical ways are available to get you around town.

Adventure Scooter & Bicycle Rentals is one of the best and largest purveyors of rental equipment, with more than 300 of each type of vehicle available. It has 10 locations around town. Bicycles come complete with baskets and locks; baby seats are also in stock. Scooters can accommodate single or double riders. Call 305-293-9933 or 305-296-5552. Always ask if they have package deals or weekend rates.

A public bus runs in town, operated by the City of Key West Transportation. Buses run weekdays, generally from 6:00 A.M. to 9:00 P.M. On Saturdays, Sunday, and holidays the buses start between 8:30 A.M. and 9:30 A.M. The bus has more than 180 stops on two routes—the Red Route and the Blue Route. It also operates a park-and-ride shuttle for those visitors who park in the city lot between Caroline and Eaton streets. The small buses leave downtown from the corner of Eaton and Duval or from Duval just north of Truman, approximately once every hour. Pick up a schedule, as the bus is not exactly prompt and waiting for almost an hour can get old in the blazing summer sun. Also, as the brochure states, "Please be aware that weather and traffic conditions may affect this schedule."

The adult fare is 75¢ (senior citizens travel for 35¢); carry exact change as the drivers don't. Children under five ride free. You can purchase a monthly pass if you're staying awhile. The bus can take you out to Stock Island as well as to many locations in Key West. I have found the drivers to be friendly and helpful. When I recently missed my stop on Stock Island, the driver turned around and took me back.

For a schedule, call 305-293-6435 or 305-292-8160, or pick one up on the bus. For special-needs transportation call 305-293-8315.

# Southernmost Shuttle of Key West

On a related note: as I've said before, you don't need a car in Key West and you'll be doing the environment and the residents a favor if you don't bring one. Parking is somewhat restricted and many of the streets are narrow.

If you're visiting Key West from the Miami area, a shuttle bus departs Miami International Airport twice every afternoon, and departs Key West twice every morning. Buses have bathrooms, TVs, and VCRs and are air-conditioned. All pick-ups in Miami are at ground transportation on the airport's lower level. All drop-offs are at major Key West hotels and airport terminals. You can purchase either a one-way or round-trip ticket. Fares are reasonable; the trip takes approximately four hours, traffic permitting. For schedules and reservations, call 800-390-7176 daily between 9:00 A.M. and 5:00 P.M.

# Lloyd's Original Key West Nature Bike Tours

Like so many before him, Lloyd Mager came to Key West in the 1970s but likes to believe he was "born here . . . in a much less expensive time." For six years, he has led leisurely nature-related bike tours around his island to "enjoy the moment, taste a mango, drink a coconut," and more. He often has 20 or 25 people on a tour.

Key West is the perfect town for bikes, which tend to be no-speed and painted pink. You'll even see many old-time bicycles around town; locals call these Conch (native Key Wester) cruisers. Most people don't even wear helmets, not that I think this is a good idea. Of course, most of the side streets are blissfully empty and the streets are so flat. Mager's tour is not particularly strenuous and is appropriate for all ages.

On his two-hour bike trip, Mager makes between 15 and 20 stops, though not always the same ones and not always on the same route. "My route is based on the flowering and fruiting trees," he explains. He always stays away from the main streets. He may take you down Galveston Lane, "a secret rendezvous area." Or he may take you to the Jewish side of the town's cemetery, which has a cherry-covered hedge ripe with fruit in the early spring. Or he may stop to introduce you to a few of the local characters, like cemetery manager William Gates, a fifth-generation Conch.

"This is a slice-of-life field trip, uncommercialized," says Mager. "It's not contrived. I wanted to share my lifestyle; it's synonymous with Key West." Read: laid-back.

Tours are held every day except Monday. Tuesday through Saturday they begin at 9:00 A.M. and at 3:00 P.M. On Sunday there is one tour only, at 10:30 A.M. The cost ($15.00 recently) is slightly higher if you also rent a bike. To sign up, call Mager at 305-294-1882, reserve a spot, and meet at the downtown Moped Hospital located at the corner of Truman and Simonton.

# Key West Afoot

You're new to Key West and you don't like the looks of all the T-shirt shops on Duval Street. This isn't why you came to this island paradise.

The *real* Key West, where people live, raise children, and tend gardens and cats and dogs, is not on Duval. It's on the side streets and tiny cul-de-sacs. Some of them are quite difficult to find. Without a map, you may go around and around.

For those of you who believe the best way to get around is on your own steam, I recommend a walking tour. George Fontana, who also owns Abaco Inn and has led walking tours around the world (to places like Fiji, Machu Picchu, and Alaska), has been offering tours of Key West for 14 years. He will meet you at a designated spot and take you as far as you want to go. Fontana especially loves the back streets with picturesque names like Galveston Lane and Lovers' Lane, pointing out the famous writers' homes and colonies, the Cuban and cigarmakers' architecture, and the huge variety of flowering trees, shrubs, and smaller plants. He often includes a special garden stop, too. He walks at a leisurely pace, and it is obvious he loves his town. A former Bostonian who moved south and never looked back, he is often asked why he's so mellow. "I live in Key West," is answer enough.

Most tours last approximately one hour, and the price is $30.00 for one or two walkers. Add $5.00 for each additional pedestrian. Fontana can take from 1 to 20 on a walk. Due to the heat, walks are generally in the morning or the late afternoon.

**For more information:** Key West Afoot, 415 Julia Street, Key West, FL 33040. Call 305-296-2212.


# Audubon House and Tropical Gardens

Audubon House, a historic home, offers a clearly narrated, self-guided tour of the home of sea captain John Geiger and its exquisite gardens. In 1831 and 1832, John James Audubon visited the Dry Tortugas and the Geiger family in Key West and sketched 18 native birds while here. In 1996, this site was voted the best museum in the Keys by *South Florida Magazine*.

The home, a restored wooden structure built in 1832, is one of the oldest in the city. It has three floors of period antiques and 28 original engravings by Audubon. Among these are the white-crowned pigeon, the turkey buzzard, the scarlet ibis, the roseate spoonbill, and a pair of peregrine falcons.

The large, orderly garden is a primary attraction in Key West. It is a formal garden of mostly South American plants, both useful and ornamental exotics, kept in excellent shape by a full-time gardener. She is often on the premises to answer questions. Of particular note are dozens of orchids, which are tied onto trees and eventually attach themselves; a splendid example of a Geiger tree, named for John Geiger who first brought it to Key West; an Audubon tree, named in honor of Audubon who used it as a background for his pipery flycatcher–gray kingbird engraving; a Key lime tree; a prominent autograph tree, an endangered native of the Keys, with many carved initials and names (the sturdy leaves of these trees were once used as notepaper, postcards, and playing cards); a butterfly garden; an herb garden; and much, much more. The cast-iron "Child's Fountain," dated 1872, hails from Kensington Gardens, England. The plantings are bordered by black 19th-century beer bottles, found under the house during its restoration in 1959, placed neck down. This was an old Southern tradition. Benches are provided for sitting, reading, writing, or daydreaming.

The small gift shop carries tasteful cards, books, and original, first-edition lithographs by Audubon. Office parties, receptions, and weddings are often held in this pastoral setting, one of the prettiest on the island.

The Audubon House and Gardens is located at the corner of Whitehead and Greene streets, on the gulf side, near Mallory Square. Whitehead runs parallel to Duval and is a more quiet, beautiful, and much less commercial street. The museum and its grounds are open daily from 9:30 A.M. to 5:00 P.M.; admission is charged.

*For more information:* Call 305-294-2116.

## Casa Antigua

It's well-known that Ernest Hemingway lived in Key West. He wrote many of his bestselling and most popular works—*Death in the Afternoon*, *The Green Hills of Africa*, and *To Have and Have Not*—here. Some people on the island still remember him, a bear of a man whom many called an early hippie. Parts of *To Have and Have Not* concern his life and friends in Key West.

Hemingway's longtime home, at 907 Whitehead Street, is one of the top tourist attractions on the island. But aside from the numerous resident polydactyl cats, rumored to be descendants of Papa's several polydactyl cats, this is not an especially natural spot. However, Hemingway's first home on Key West does involve nature. It is the lovely Casa Antigua, which now boasts a historic tropical garden and a tourist shop with a tacky name, The Pelican Poop Shoppe, but quite good local and Haitian merchandise. It's the interior garden you really want to see.

The building was erected in 1919 as a hotel and car dealership. In April 1928, Hemingway and his second wife, Pauline, first traveled to Key West, arriving by ocean liner. They planned to pick up a Ford he had ordered and drive back up north. The Ford was late, and the Hemingways stayed at the hotel, then called the Trev-Mor Hotel, for seven weeks, waiting for the car to arrive. During this time, the author wrote *A Farewell to Arms* in these rooms, and the Hemingways fell in love with Key West. Hemingway made it his winter home for approximately nine years.

The small, tropically exotic garden with palms and orchids is pretty; it is in the middle of an indoor courtyard, with balconies on all four sides. You can't go into his rooms, although local gossip has it that may become a possibility. A pond and a nice parrot complete this small piece of local history.

Self-guided tours are available daily between 10:00 A.M. and 6:00 P.M.; admission is $2.00.

*For more information:* The Casa Antigua, 314 Simonton Street, Key West, FL 33040. Call 303-292-9955.

# *Discovery* Glass-Bottom Boat

Before I booked passage on one of the large glass-bottom boats, the *Discovery*, docked in Key West at the end of Margaret Street to the right of Mallory Square, I expected I would find a large boat with a glass floor through which to see fish and coral and more. Wrong. After gaining some distance from shore, we entered the underwater viewing room. Glass windows are all around the center of the boat. We saw hundreds of colorful orange, blue, and blackfish, and coral formations in a variety of shapes. The trip was expertly narrated throughout.

A bit about this particular boat: the *Discovery* was built in Jacksonville. Its length is 78 feet; its passenger capacity is 124. The boat has 20 windows in the sides of the hull, which are at a 45-degree angle to the ocean's bottom. It has an upper deck and a lower deck; the main room or salon is air-conditioned.

The first activity is an upper-deck water tour of Old Town Key West harbor, including Fort Zachary Taylor, the old U.S. Navy submarine pens, and a few islands. Then, we sailed for 30 minutes to the living coral reef six miles off shore. We went to the lower deck for about a half hour, during which the narration was nonstop, based on exactly what we saw. We went back to the upper deck for the return to Key West harbor.

Two words of caution: As we left the Key West shore, it was a windy day and the sea was a bit choppy, so the boat did rock somewhat. I had to hang on to the handrails; I imagine some passengers felt seasick. And, once you're down in the glassed-in viewing room of the boat, try to get a seat as close as possible to the windows. If you hope to capture large fish images, I'd recommend bringing a telephoto lens.

The boat has adequate bathrooms and snacks. There's even wine and beer, if you desire. The boat also makes a Champagne Sunset Trip, which includes complimentary bubbly.

My recent trip was well worth the money; I'd go back on this particular boat in a flash, although I can't speak for all the similar excursions that are offered up and down the Keys. This is a relaxing and educational way to spend two hours. If you will never go scuba diving or snorkeling, this is the only way I know to get under the water while feeling totally protected, safe, and dry.

*For more information:* The *Discovery* Glass-Bottom Boat, 251 Margaret Street, Key West, FL 33040. Call 305-293-0099.

# Key West Aquarium

The Key West Aquarium, the island's first attraction, opened to the public in 1934 for the convenience of railroad passengers during the Great Depression. At that time, Key West was 100 percent on relief, turning its charter over to the state and federal governments. Governor Julius Stone, appointed Florida administrator of the Federal Emergency Relief Administration, oversaw a community planning experiment promoting Key West as *the* tourist resort of the American Tropics. The aquarium construction from 1932 to 1934 was a major part of the city's attempt to make an economic recovery by becoming a tourist destination. Workers, employed by the Federal Emergency Relief Administration, constructed the building, located on the beachfront just in front of Mallory Square, by pouring cement in forms one bucket at a time.

Open daily between 10:00 A.M. and 6:00 P.M., it still is one of the top tourist attractions in Key West. Along with its clearly labeled displays and its shark feedings, the aquarium has participated in the Green Sea Turtle Head Start program, raising baby turtles in captivity for their first year. Today, two green sea turtles and many other marine animals call the aquarium home because their injuries prevent them from living in the wild.

Some of the creatures you will see, and maybe even touch, are sharks, barracuda, tarpon, jacks, sawfish, stingrays, and snooks. Glassed-in tanks line the walls of the building interior. The facility specializes in animals and fish indigenous to the area, including sharks, turtles, and tropical and game fish. The 50,000-gallon Atlantic Shores Exhibit in the rear of the aquarium simulates a mangrove habitat near shore and reef. Most days, you will see curious wild heron, ibises, or pelicans on its fences, watching you watch the marine show.

In a tidal pool, you can touch a queen conch, a sea squirt, a starfish, or a sea anemone. Maybe stroking a horseshoe crab appeals to you more.

Aside from offering daily tours led by enthusiastic leaders, the aquarium hosts educational programs for thousands of schoolchildren each year, helping to educate them about the fragile ecosystem in the Florida Keys. They present programs on migratory birds, marine mammals, coastal habitats, and more ocean-related topics.

This is not a large aquarium. Guided tours, which take between 30 and 45 minutes, are offered four times a day, at 11:00 A.M., 1:00 P.M., 2:00 P.M., and 4:30 P.M.

This is one of the better activities in Key West to do with kids, a great one for a rainy day. Call ahead for prices, which are subject to change.

*For more information:* Key West Aquarium, 1 Whitehead Street at Mallory Square, Key West, FL 33040. Call 305-296-2051.

# Key West Beaches

I'm not a beach person. I find hanging out on the sand, ogling human bodies, and lying prone for hours a boring activity. Listening to loud boom boxes or having sand kicked into my lunch does not make my day. But I do enjoy swimming, and that's one reason I go to the beach occasionally. Beaches are enticing in the Keys year-round; the water is always bath temperature, at the minimum.

That said, by far my favorite beach in Key West is **Fort Zachary Taylor.** Even though you have to pay a small admission price, the 1,000-foot beach is far more beautiful and less crowded than the other slightly rowdy beaches. A state historic site, it includes a fortification begun in 1845, just after Florida became a state. It was occupied by Captain John Brannon and remained in Union hands throughout the war. Here you can see a display of artifacts and models of original guns and facilities; several Civil War cannons are on display. Guided tours are available. The area has an Australian pine forest in which you can sit, picnic, and read once you've had enough sun. This is also the best place to watch the sunset, Mallory Square notwithstanding. (The sunset viewing is good there, too, but, it feels more like an amusement park than an appreciation of nature.) Final points in Fort Taylor's favor are the good snorkeling; several outside showers; the convenient concession stand, picnic tables, and grills; and the fact that it is extremely popular with the locals.

The entrance to the fort is through Southard Street to Truman Annex, now a community of upscale condos and amazingly quiet streets. The beach is open from 8:00 A.M. to sunset. Some guest houses and hotels will lend you an entrance pass that enables you to get onto the beach for free. Call 305-292-6713 for hours.

I also like the small **South Beach,** at the bottom of Duval Street where it intersects South Street. It's just past the Southernmost House, situated in front of South Beach Seafood & Raw Bar, Key West's only oceanfront raw bar, and a good open restaurant with a terrace. (Please note that this beach and restaurant were quite badly damaged during Hurricane Georges; hopefully, by the time of this book's printing, the beach and the restaurant will be back to their beautiful selves.) Tennessee Williams used to bicycle over and swim at South Beach frequently, often in the nude. Although it's a tiny beach with no facilities, it's a good place to work on a tan, to walk far out into the ocean, and to watch fish jump at insects or pelicans dive-bomb for fish. Often an elegant great blue heron strides around seeking its next meal as the less graceful and more comical pelicans crash against the waves.

The longest beach on the island is **Smathers**, just west of the Key West International Airport on A-1A (South Roosevelt Boulevard). You can park your vehicle here; eat tacos, ice cream, or hot dogs; and rent Windsurfers, rafts, or parasails. Rest rooms are available, as is an outdoor shower. Across the street are row after row of condominiums. People often play volleyball on this beach. It is also favored by many students on spring break. This is a great place to see the tiniest bathing suits imaginable, on people of all ages and sizes, male and female.

**Clarence C. Higgs Memorial Beach** (also known locally as Memorial or County Beach) is next to White Street Pier, which was recently renovated and cleaned up. Families tend to congregate here for the playground, picnic tables, and small restaurant. Free tennis courts are across the street. Adjacent to the beach, if you tire of swimming or sunbathing, is the West Martello Tower and Garden Center. This beach is on Atlantic Boulevard near the south end of White Street, half a mile west of Smathers Beach.

I like Smathers and Higgs best early in the morning when you can pick up a Cuban breakfast on White Street and eat it in the sand or sitting at a covered table while gulls try to steal your crusty bread. Across the street from Smathers is a good birding spot, the Riggs Wildlife Refuge, with a small observation deck. Although serene, it's also a bit run-down and, quite frankly, doesn't feel entirely safe.

Finally, what's a visit to Key West without stopping at **Dog Beach**? Key West loves its pets so much that it has given over a tiny beach just to the dogs. The dogs no longer need to suffer the summer sun. This rocky shoreline is just to the right of the famous and fine Louie's Backyard restaurant and tiny waterfront bar at 700 Waddell Street. Dog Beach is where the locals take their hot pooches to cool off. It's not a place you'd care to do much swimming or sunbathing, but if you like nature in the form of wet, wiggly dogs, this is a fun place to spend part of an afternoon. To get there, from Duval go down to the ocean, turn left on South Street, then right on Vernon Street. Dog Beach is at the corner of Vernon and Waddell Avenue; you can't miss it. Although there's no sign, you'll see wet dogs and Louie's Backyard. Louie's is also highly recommended, but make reservations well in advance.

# Mallory Square

Mallory Square is the only place I have visited where the sunset is worshiped. Every evening, rain or shine, winter or summer, just before the sun goes down, a huge celebration occurs here. But the main event isn't really the sunset. It's the people. First, there are the performers—for example, a man who can balance shopping carts on his chin, another who trains cats to jump through hoops, a third who has a performing potbellied pig, an Uncle Sam–type character, a tightrope walker. Then, there are the concessionaires—the Cookie Lady with her loud, piercing voice; popcorn carts; and jewelry and T-shirt makers galore. A few fortune-tellers or tarot card readers are generally ready to look into your future. (Prediction: more sun, if you're here for a while.)

On a recent trip, I watched a bagpipe player, browsed the tables of inexpensive souvenirs, mostly jewelry and hand-painted T-shirts, and ordered popcorn, the most expensive I've ever eaten at $3.00 a bag but hardly the best.

The most interesting people are those standing around you—generally hundreds from around the world—people of all colors, shapes, ages, and sizes, the majority of whom are toting cameras or video recorders, wearing T-shirts, and clapping when the sun finally goes down.

This event is worth attending, but only once or twice unless you enjoy a zoolike atmosphere. Some visitors find it claustrophobic. The quality and quantity of the acts have gone down, too, in the past two years because the Hilton Resort and Marina, to the city dock's left, has hired away some of the best acts to entertain its customers.

I prefer Mallory Square as a great spot to enjoy an early morning coffee. I stop at Nestors at 300 Fitzpatrick Street, buy a Cuban cafe con leche (some of the best on the island), and head down to sit on the dock. Usually one or two fishers are there before me, feeding bait or small catch to comical, waddling pelicans. The fascinating views include Tank Island, recently developed for luxury housing, and boats ranging from small fishing craft to huge cruise ships. Oftentimes, a bold great blue heron walks calmly around the dock, keeping a respectable distance, and several skinny, homeless cats scurry out to pick up crumbs left from the night before or from the morning's bagels or muffins.

Mallory Square sits on the former docks where the Mallory Steamship Line once tied up. The area was named in the 1960s for native son Stephen R. Mallory, once Jefferson Davis's Confederate secretary of the navy and a U.S. senator. This was the heart of the salvage and wrecking industry in the 19th century. You can still visit a warehouse where you can buy native sponges and one filled with shells. Don't overlook the Waterfront Playhouse, circa 1850, once used for storing items salvaged from ships and a waiting auction. It's now the site of some Broadway-quality theater. The old wooden piers were renovated first in 1963 and later for cruise ships, which visit here most of the year. However, one strictly-enforced rule about the sunset performance is that all cruise ships must move beyond the view when the sun disappears below the horizon.

To get to Mallory Square, head north down Whitehead Street—or Duval Street—until you're almost at the water. Mallory Square is behind and to the right of the Key West Aquarium, to the left of the Waterfront Playhouse.

## Mangrove Mistress

You can get out onto the water in the lower Keys in a multitude of ways. Several chartered excursions include lively talks about the area, and free beer and wine, as much as you care to drink. But few of these trips provide commentary on the wildlife and sealife in these waters, or an environmentally sound approach to nature. Who wants to go out in a loud motorboat, on jet skis, or with a pack of tourists who believe the ultimate thrill is to get drunk out in the middle of the ocean?

Lynda Schuh of Key West operates one of the best boating opportunities in the lower Keys. Her *Mangrove Mistress* is a shallow-draft 30-foot Tennessee river cruiser with a small, quiet motor. She can take you out for a half day or a whole day, into the backcountry to places you'd never find on your own—or, for that matter, on most of the sailboats or catamarans that leave from Key West harbor.

Schuh knows her stuff. She's offered these trips for 11 years. A transplant from Michigan, where she worked in the restaurant trade, Schuh has made it her second career to help protect nature in the Keys and to run trips for those who feel the same way or are willing to consider a new perspective. When she's not leading environmental tours, she might be volunteering at Wildlife Rescue of the Florida Keys, where she feeds injured birds and trains other volunteers. She is knowledgeable and careful about where she goes. She wouldn't dream of feeding or getting close to a dolphin. She respects their space and knows that touching and feeding wild animals is generally detrimental to the creatures. She gives all creatures wide berths. Her boat has no sound system, no alcohol. It's just you, a couple of fellow passengers, and the big, wide water.

One day in May—it was 85 degrees with drippingly high humidity—I joined three other women and Schuh for a four-hour afternoon cruise in Great White Heron Refuge in the Gulf of Mexico. She explained her philosophy right up front: "No taking, no touching. Don't harm anything. The only things we might take are plastic fishing line or injured birds." (She even carries cages on board for that purpose.) We were quite protected from the sun, and we had several opportunities to snorkel. Miles out into the gulf, we hardly felt the high humidity; it was at least 10 degrees cooler than on land. Replenished with the fresh water, fresh pineapple, sea breezes, and silence, we had drifted into a quieter, saner world. During our trip, we often looked both up and down; Schuh pointed out fish, birds, and plants with equal pleasure. She offered the clearest explanation of the three types of mangroves that I have heard. (See sidebar on page 95.) She often spoke to the birds, calling them beauties.

On that hot afternoon, we saw parrot fish, little least terns, osprey and bald eagle nests, cormorants, sponge algae, tunicats (a common marine invertebrate), and great white and little blue herons. Schuh told us she sometimes sees raccoons swimming between the mangrove islands at low tide.

The highlight of the trip was spotting two dolphins leap and dive, about 20 feet off our boat. We were thankful to see dolphins in the wild, not in captivity. Unfortunately, another group that Schuh said billed itself as an ecology tour—a group on jet skis, no less—disturbed the tranquillity we shared with the dolphins.

By the middle of our trip, without access to a map or a great sense of direction, I felt disoriented but not in the least bit fearful. I had no idea where we were; I could see no buildings or distinguishing natural features. But I knew we'd return to shore safely. Schuh uses a compass, buoy markers, and her memory to make these lengthy trips out in the water. She has several routes that she travels regularly.

Schuh's boat can accommodate from four to six adults. The craft's amenities include snorkeling equipment, nature books, first-aid supplies, a cellular phone for emergencies, life preservers, a toilet, a shower, a shade canopy, an ice cooler with water and soft drinks, pretzels, and fruit, plus binoculars for bird-watching.

Schuh books her limited number of seats in advance, especially during peak tourist season, and doesn't go out if the weather is threatening. The day of our trip the sky became black but the rains didn't come down until the tail end of our journey. She requires reservations and accepts cash, traveler's checks, or personal checks for her tours. She is more than happy to provide a family or private group tour and often offers women-only trips.

Schuh offers two trips daily: one in the morning, another in the afternoon, for three and a half or four hours. Her boat is moored north of Key West, at Murray Marina near College Road on Route 1. It's past Stock Island, and the local McDonald's, if you decide to drive or bicycle. If you're on foot, a city bus will drop you there.

Because all the local water-based excursions are somewhat costly, it pays to shop around. For my money, Schuh's is the best I've taken. The trip is what she promotes it to be: environmentally educational and relaxing. Just what I want out there in the vast, mysterious open waters.

*For more information:* Lynda Schuh, *Mangrove Mistress,* 841 Cherokee Street, Sugarloaf Key, FL 33042. Call 305-294-4213 or 305-745-8886.

---

# Mangroves

Three species of mangroves, trees and shrubs that are adapted to grow in loose, salty soil, exist in the Florida Keys. Not everyone finds them beautiful, but some do. Alison Lurie once described them as "low gray-green mangrove islands float[ing] on the horizon like vegetable whales." Rachel Carson liked them, too, describing the mangrove forests of the Keys as "silent, mysterious, always changing." Most of these are obvious because of their dramatic aerial root system, unlike any other I've seen. Mangroves are the primary trees in tropical estuarine and saltwater habitats. In the ecosystem, their purpose is to trap sediment and absorb nutrients, which helps clean offshore water.

The red mangrove, sometimes called the "walking tree," is the most common on the ocean side of the mangrove forests. Its network of roots extends from the trunk, penetrating the soil below the tree. It has leathery leaves and small yellow flowers that appear in spring and summer, after which the tree produces cigar-shaped seedlings of up to 11 inches that then float away in the water. The red mangrove is an important part of the Key deer's diet, and it also feeds and protects young fish, spiny lobsters, and pink shrimp.

The large black mangrove also has a system of shallow cable roots that radiate outward both laterally and vertically. These trees have aerial roots that extend above the mud almost eight inches, forming what looks like a spongy carpet. Their dark green leaves are often encrusted with salt, turning them almost white. The tree produces fragrant white flowers in spring and early summer, and later, seedlings that look like chubby lima beans. This mangrove is sometimes found on an island where the red mangroves are absent, but it generally forms the middle belt of trees in the mangrove forest system.

On the innermost band of the mangrove forest is the white mangrove, usually found in dry or nearly dry areas. With broad oval leaves, this mangrove has no aerial roots.

Buttonwoods, although not true mangroves, are also salt-tolerant trees commonly found in mangrove forests. Historically, their wood was used to produce charcoal for cooking. They flower in the summer and produce a buttonlike seed case. Mangrove seed pods were once used to create jewelry. The pods were dried, sliced, and strung.

Mangrove forests are incredibly diverse due to the fish, birds, and other wildlife living within them. Many reef fish, including pink shrimp, snapper, and snook, use mangrove communities as nurseries. Mangrove forests act as buffers against waves, and they shelter other trees and even property during tropical storms.

Mangroves are threatened by human waste runoff, oil and pesticide contamination, and their use as dump sites. Trimming of the trees by residents, and, of course, the occasional hurricane can cause extensive damage. However, the trees are hardy and can quite easily propagate in the powerful Keys' sunlight.

Under the Mangrove Protection Act of 1985, it is illegal to destroy or damage mangroves in Florida. They are considered a species of special concern throughout the entire state.

*Mangrove Tree*

# MARC Plant Outlet

If you're looking for a potted plant for a relative or friend while staying in Key West, the best place to do so is at the MARC Plant Outlet at 812 Southard Street. MARC, which has existed for 30 years, stands for the Monroe Association for Retarded Citizens. The outlet is staffed primarily by men and women from the organization's sheltered workshop. Fifty percent of the plants sold by MARC are grown at the facility, and the other 50 percent come from the mainland. Approximately 40 percent of the plants sold here are native, the rest exotic.

Walk in and admire the healthy, bright plants. For sale are lantana, poinsettia, a variety of palms and orchids, bromeliads, hibiscus, passionflowers, ferns, and several bedding plants. It's always strange to me, somehow, to see petunias, impatiens, and begonias, which I think of as northern plants, in Key West. But, like so many species, they can be grown year-round here. Also available are fertilizers, imaginative pots and baskets, and gardening tools.

During the holiday season, they sell Christmas trees, too. (Conchs love to decorate for the winter season, but they pay steep prices for these real northern trees.)

MARC offers six annual workshops in its horticultural education series, including free lectures on such topics as bromeliads, orchids, and palms. These are scheduled on Saturdays for up to two hours and are advertised in the local newspapers.

To find MARC, in Old Town head north on Duval, Whitehead, or Simonton and take a right on Southard. Proceed to the corner of Margaret and Southard streets. The outlet is housed outside the large, brick Old Harris School. The outlet is open every day except Sunday.

*For more information:* Call manager Mark Lindas, 305-296-9556.

# More Key West Parks and Gardens

## *Charles "Sonny" McCoy Indigenous Park*

Charles "Sonny" McCoy Indigenous Park boasts the largest public collection of tropical native plants in the Keys. Many gardeners here care passionately if plants are native or exotic, i.e, imported. The park offers more than 125 species of trees and shrubs and several roaming feral chickens and roosters. Among the many trees are torchwood, saffron plum, pitch apple, and lignum vitae. You'll also see the autograph tree; its leaves are so tough and leathery that people write on them, leaving messages for the next viewers. (Another fine autograph tree can be seen at the Audubon House.) Several tropical fruit trees grow here as well, breadfruit, Spanish lime, and sour orange among them.

In the spring and fall, several songbirds—for example, buntings, tanagers, and more than 20 species of warblers—visit the park, which also provides habitat for several species of large, brightly colored butterflies. These might be giant swallowtails, red admirals, or zebra longwings.

The park also houses the Wildlife Rescue of the Florida Keys, which rehabilitates wild birds and small creatures (see Index).

The garden is named for Charles "Sonny" McCoy, mayor of Key West in the late 1970s. He is especially famous for water-skiing to Havana Harbor in 6 hours and 10 minutes as part of a 1978 international goodwill campaign that went to Cuba. For his effort, he received President Jimmy Carter's best wishes.

To get to the garden, from the south end of Duval Street, take a right on Truman Avenue or one of its parallel streets and walk down White Street almost to the White Street Pier. The park is across the street from the newly refurbished pier, on your left as you face the ocean. It is open Monday through Friday from 7:00 A.M. to 4:00 P.M.; self-guided tours are available on request.

*For more information:* Call 305-292-8155. Self-guided tours can be arranged at 305-292-8157.

## The Medicine Garden

In early 1997, I felt a tremendous urge to meditate and calm my life, and what better place than at the small, lovely Medicine Garden on a side street in Old Town. I had never heard of this idyllic spot before my 1997 winter stay in the Keys. When I saw a calendar listing for a talk by a Buddhist monk and a meditation session, I knew this was something I needed to explore.

The garden, located at 800 Amelia Street, perpendicular to Duval Street at the south end of town, is not hard to find. Bamboo gates and a small sign indicate you have arrived. Such silence. Signs say, "Please whisper in the garden." On the night I attended wandering Sri Lankan monk Bhante Wimala's lecture, approximately 100 people of all ages and nationalities joined me in utter tranquillity for almost two hours. Incense and candles burned and the scent of flowers filled the air as we listened to this traveling monk in a long saffron robe explain the basic tenets of Buddhism. He helped us meditate together. My only complaint is that the chairs were not exactly comfortable, but this lack of comfort is important for some meditation practices.

Aside from providing a quiet place to sit, the round coral rock garden is lovely to look at, with hanging crystals, philodendrons, and trunks of Caribbean driftwood. Cacti, a variety of palms, hibiscus, Angel's trumpets, and succulents surround the calm space. Animal and Buddha sculptures fill the garden, and a delightful small pond with carp and a sound of waterfalls is restful. Many gourds hang in the trees for birds to nest in. The garden, begun six years ago by John Hillman (also known as Pejuda), is open during daylight hours for quiet sitting. Pejuda, who is originally from Texas, sees his role as a caretaker of the garden. Meditation, Buddhist, and "all-path" teaching workshops and discussions are regularly held on Wednesday, Thursday, and Friday evenings. There is no entrance fee, but a money box for contributions to garden maintenance is at the gate. No food, drinks, or smoking are allowed; volunteers are always welcome.

*For more information:* 800 Amelia Street, Key West, FL 33040. Call 305-294-5818.

## Key West Botanical Garden Society Garden

Located near the community college on Stock Island, Key West Botanical Garden Society Garden is accessible by bus or by bike, and is situated on six acres that include one of the last two undeveloped native hardwood hammocks in the Key West area. Lots of exotic and even champion trees are here, but quite honestly, I was disappointed. The brochure rack for self-guided tours was empty; many trees were not adequately labeled or were identified only with very small tags, the trail was slightly unkempt, and not many flowers were in bloom. Although this is an important property, it is not the most satisfying garden spot in Key West.

That said, many trees and other vegetation here should interest the plant lover. Included in these are a clump of cabbage palms, a green buttonwood thicket, and three Florida Champion trees: the Arjan almond, the barringtonia, and the Cuban lignum vitae, which is endangered. Champion status is determined by a point system that assesses the height, the trunk's circumference, the crown spread, and the overall condition of the tree. Among other beauties are the large mahogany, the wild coffee shrub with its red berries, the gumbo limbo, and the small Venezuelan rose tree with an orange brushlike blossom. One palm grove is named for Colonel J. P. Scurlock, writer of the excellent *Native Trees and Shrubs of the Florida Keys*, who lived on Sugarloaf Key for 22 years.

To get to the garden, go north from Key West along Route 1 (out Truman Avenue) to Stock Island and turn left onto College Road. Go past the community college. The garden, which charges no admission, is off Aquino Circle next to Bay Shore Manor. Free parking is available. If you'd like to help beautify the garden, volunteer work parties meet here Saturday mornings at 9:00 A.M.

*For more information:* Call 305-294-5426.


## The Monroe County Library Palm Garden

The pink stucco Monroe County library at 700 Fleming Street is one of my favorite places in Key West. The atmosphere is comfortable and relaxing, and the library's collections—especially of Florida writers, periodicals, and video and audiotapes—are extensive. The staff is helpful and low-key. Tom Hambright, the Florida historian, is a dynamo of information and enthusiasm. One highlight on the first Saturday of every month during the winter season is the Friends of the Library's outdoor book sale. They also sponsor an excellent lecture series, with the likes of poet Richard Wilbur and author Joy Williams reading.

The book sales are held in the public palm garden next to the library, which opened in June 1994. Formerly a patch of lawn, it is now known for its approximately 60 palms of 30 species, its shade, and its seats. It's a great place to write, read, or pet a wandering cat. The garden was designed by Patrick Tierney, a landscape artist who lives in North Miami Beach. He and the Friends of the Library Association came up with the garden concept in 1993. The library donated the land for the garden, and the philanthropic Rath Foundation pledged to maintain the garden for the first 10 years. The Rath Foundation commemorates V. Duane Rath, a steel magnate who had a winter home here.

The one-eighth-acre site includes mostly what are called "survival palms," either native or well suited to the tropical conditions. Two royal palms flank the garden's entrance; these can grow up to 90 feet tall. Other plants on-site include a Puerto Rican hat palm; a buccaneer palm, an Everglades palm, a pygmy date, a large Spanish lime tree, sabal palms (the state tree), and several bushes and grasses. The gates to the garden are open Monday through Saturday during library hours.

*For more information:* Monroe County May Hill Russell Library, 700 Fleming Street, Key West, FL 33040. Call 305-292-3595.

## Little Hamaca Park

Little Hamaca Park has been a wildlife sanctuary and was almost turned into a complex of condominiums. Saved from that fate in 1991, it now is a small park with a boardwalk. Now Little Hamaca is primarily a birding spot, so the best time to go is in early morning. The trails through buttonwoods and mangroves often afford views of a variety of waders and land birds. Nearby are salt ponds, where residents once evaporated seawater to collect salt. You can sometimes see ducks, rails, and roseate spoonbills at the salt ponds.

The park gates are open from 7:00 A.M. to sunset and entry is free. On South Roosevelt, make a left turn on Flagler Street. Turn left at the park sign onto Government Road. You will be near the airport.

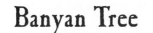

# Banyan Tree

If you haven't seen one of the gigantic banyan trees, with gray bark and a huge system of external roots, you're in for a pleasant surprise. Actually, banyan is not a species, but rather, any East Indian tree that has multiple trunks attached to a single plant. The

Indian banyan is named for Hindu traders called Banyans; this tree is sacred to the Hindus. In India, one has been measured at 2,000-feet-by-85-feet high! In the Florida Keys, the evergreen banyans are one of two ficuses: the strangler fig or the short-leafed fig. Most common in the Keys is the strangler fig.

Anywhere they grow, the banyan trees are amazing, often spreading across driveways, across streets, across yards. They frequently grow to 70 or 100 feet. Three especially prominent specimens can be found in Key West alone. One is right in front of the Banyan Resort at 323 Whitehead Street, not far from the Ernest Hemingway House. Although signs posted on the tree forbid touching and make it difficult to photograph without obstruction, it's a thing of natural beauty. Another is directly in front of the Key West Lighthouse at 938 Whitehead. The third is next to Nancy's William Street Guesthouse at 329 William Street at the intersection of Eaton Street.

You'll see examples of these trees throughout the Keys. Admire these huge wonders.

---

# Mosquito Coast Island Outfitters and Kayak Guides

Sea kayaking is a popular activity in the Keys. Often the water is calm, and there are endless fascinating sights to see way out in the water that you'd never possibly see on terra firma.

If you're a novice to kayaking or snorkeling, and you need a bit of help and encouragement, one outfit with a fine reputation is Mosquito Coast, owned and run by Dan and Ellie McConnell of Key West. They provide guided, backcountry tours for both novices and experienced boaters and snorkelers. No experience is necessary; their kayaks are of advanced design, stable, and versatile.

Trips are open to almost all ages; older people are especially encouraged. A child under nine is not appropriate for these trips; young children over nine are welcome when accompanied by an adult.

One or two groups go out daily, depending on season and weather. Dan McConnell has four guides on staff, and he takes up the overflow. His guides are chosen for "people skills, sensitivity, [being] good sailors, and all know[ing] the Latin names [of trees, shells, fish, etc.]." (Don't worry, they also know the English names.) The kayaks launch at Geiger and Sugarloaf Key. You meet in the early morning at the Duval Street shop, which doubles as a wine bar (he's got a great selection of French wines), and drive to Boca Chica in the company van.

Dan believes operating a sea kayak can be learned by novices in five minutes. The crew provides a paddle-safety talk, then hands participants life jackets, drinking water, and snacks, but not a full lunch, so you may choose to bring more food. They always stay nearby in the water. About 80 percent of the time, kayakers are in their boats; about 20 percent they may be snorkeling or walking the hard-bottom shore. Not all mangrove islands are walkable.

These trips are scientific and lots of fun. For example, explains Dan, "We talk about nutrients and reproductivity. We tell them about pelagic and superpelagic fish—tarpon, marlin, sailfish. We see whatever's there, depending on the food that's available. Sometimes we see soldier tarpon eat mangrove snapper." He does extensive research by reading and taking university classes and then passes it along to his guides. "I document my information for guides. We have a lot of show-and-tells—I consider the world a big outdoor museum. We keep improving what we do."

The routes may change on a day-to-day basis but always include trips into seldom-dived areas. The McConnells carry masks and flippers, or you can bring your own.

The trips are natural-history based and anyone who wishes can snorkel in shallow water, generally only three feet. Some of the species or phenomena you might encounter are caves and solution holes, great white herons, Wurdermann's herons (only found in the Keys), snowy egrets, yellow-crowned night herons, mangrove cuckoos, and prairie warblers. Explains Dan, "Species seen depend on the tide and the time of day. You do not go near nesting areas. Sometimes you get lucky and see hawksbill turtles, an endangered species, near Buoy Flats. You see a lot of sharks, not to get you nervous. Most are harmless."

The company's mission statement reads, "Mosquito Coast is active in the support of many organizations and groups, dedicated to the education, enjoyment and protection of our natural resources." The company makes one day a month available for fund-raising efforts for conservation organizations.

You're advised to bring waterproof binoculars or a dry bag for your non-waterproof variety. Also suggested are polarized sunglasses, sunblock, a hat or cap, a swimsuit and towel, and surf shoes. Of course, cover your shoulders when you're out in the sun for this many hours. If you don't have a waterproof camera, Dan sells disposable ones at a reasonable price.

I'm not alone in recommending Mosquito Coast. It has been featured and recommended by *Conde Nast Traveler*, *Southern Living*, *Fodor's*, and more.

Once you're back, try the McConnells' ice creams at Flamingo Crossing, right next door. They're billed as tropical ice creams and sorbets in the old Cuban style—no eggs, fresh fruit, not a lot of air, all natural ingredients. Try creamy coconut or tart, refreshing Key lime. It's also one of the best spots for people-watching in town.

Mosquito Coast Island Outfitters and Kayak Guides is located at the southern end of Duval, just south of the corner of Virginia Street.

*For more information:* 1107 Duval Street, Key West, FL 33040. Call 305-294-7178. Website: www.keywest.com/cgibin/var /discover/tours/mosquito.htm.

# Nancy's Secret Garden

I'm sitting at a picnic table with an elegant floral tablecloth on it, underneath huge exotic and indigenous trees. All the plants here at Nancy Forrester's Secret Garden are in pots; if not, this close-to-an-acre lush junglelike garden would be over-ridden by now. Opened to the public in December 1994, the rainforest shade garden attracts locals and visitors from around the world because of its world-class plant collection. Especially significant are the more than 135 varieties of palms, small and huge. For example, here is one of only 15 remaining bottle palms; its origin is Mascarenes. The ornamental palm, approximately 12 feet high, is a peachy color. But one of my favorites is the old man palm, certainly named for the shaggy, golden-tan "hair" that covers the entire stem. This only grows to 15 feet, unlike the fairly common 80-foot ornamental Florida royal palm. These are exquisite examples of these seductive, evocative trees.

The garden also features huge philodendrons, elephant ears, orchids, a good collection of bromeliads, banana trees, cane begonias, and more. You'll likely see three or four lazy cats and possibly some yellow swallowtail butterflies.

Also in this cool, relaxing garden—where one can easily spend an hour or an entire day daydreaming, writing, sleeping, drinking coffee, or having a picnic lunch—are dozens of caged exotic birds, many of them large, colorful conures or cockateels, most of which talk when they want to. I instantly fell in love with a sleepy beauty named Dulce, a white umbrella cockatoo, hatched in Florida in August 1995. A volunteer told me she's sluggish in the morning and sometimes drinks coffee from Nancy's cup. On her sign it says, "I bite fingers."

Dulce stretches out her gray, lizardlike feet to me, but as much as I long to feel them, after reading the sign, I resist. Her dark eyes have a halo of light blue around them. Her vocabulary includes, "Hello. Wanna Dance? I love you. Please talk to me." I distinctly heard her say, "Hello" and "I love you." I sing "Do You Want to Dance?" and "Shall We Dance" from *The King and I* outside her cage, but she doesn't appear to recognize these popular tunes. Maybe they're just before her time. (It's OK to sing out loud to yourself in Key West; nobody bothers you, or if anyone does, they will probably join you.)

Also noteworthy in Nancy's garden are the rustic wooden cabin, which you can rent overnight, by the week, or the month, and the tasteful gallery and gift shop, tucked in the back of the garden. "Cook House," a Bahamian structure from the 1890s was moved here. A one-room artist's studio with a large screened-in porch, it is fully furnished, with air-conditioning and a TV, and can sleep up to four people. A hammock swings invitingly outside. No pets or smoking are allowed. The rates off-season and on-season vary, as they do all over the Keys. This is one of the more unusual and lush places to sleep on the island and must be deliciously romantic and stimulating to most writers and artists. A paradise in the middle of paradise. I can imagine writing poetry or a novel here.

The small gift shop and gallery specializes in local and imported art, boxes, napkins, assorted sarongs, scarves, botanical prints, and wooden toys from exotic climes like Bali, Timor, and Indonesia. It's cool, and no one pushes you to buy. Like the garden, it's restful. Sometimes the parrots are tucked in a cool corner of the gallery if you haven't seen them outside.

Nancy's Secret Garden is located at One Freeschool Lane, opposite Heron House at 512 Simonton Street. Freeschool Lane is between Southard and Fleming in the middle of Old Town. Admission is $5.00, and if you plan to return, you can purchase an individual or a family membership for a reasonable rate.
*For more information:* Call 305-294-0015.

# Wildlife Rescue of the Florida Keys

I discovered Wildlife Rescue of the Florida Keys in January 1994 when it was still located at the Turtle Kraals Restaurant, situated above tidal-flushed corrals where sea turtles were once butchered and canned. A neighbor on our street, a native Key West Cuban lady who feeds the Old Town neighborhood's feral chickens, roosters, and their peeps, came to us crying that one of the peeps was ill. She asked us to either destroy it or take it somewhere. She didn't have a car, and she didn't have the heart to kill it even though its tiny stomach had been torn open and its intestines were hanging out.

The tiny yellow chick was in terrible shape, and we quickly made some phone calls and found the Wildlife Rescue of the Florida Keys (WRFK). We promptly placed the peep in a small wicker basket and drove down. No, it didn't live, but in the process I discovered this wonderful organization and its remarkable, dedicated director, Becky Barron.

This is a sanctuary for injured birds and small animals

founded almost 20 years ago. In 1994, for example, the non-profit group cared for more than 800 birds and critters. In 1997, that number was approximately 1,000. Many of them are able to be released; a few die. The rest live here for the remainder of their lives. Among these, the day we took the peep in, were two ospreys, several pelicans, a peregrine falcon, many herring and laughing gulls, several royal and noddy terns, a large green iguana mending from a head injury, a few pigeons, and three free-ranging territorial chickens. They all were in clean cages of varying sizes with appropriate food and plenty of fresh water, all enclosed under a wire-mesh ceiling.

Since 1994, things have greatly improved for this nonprofit agency in many ways, but the summer of 1998 bought a few surprises. Until that time Becky Barron was a full-time employee, but still its only one. In November 1994, the shelter moved to its current, much more spacious home on the west side of Indigenous Park, a fitting and restful spot for wildlife. It's a green park where there are other birds, more trees, and more shade. Also, the lights of the Turtle Kraal's parking lot no longer shine on the sick and injured creatures at all hours.

Barron gathered together a loyal group of 25 volunteers, staged several flea markets and festivals as fund-raisers throughout the year, and gave workshops and talks around the Keys. She is a trained veterinary technician, an active member of Lower Keys Friends of Animals (she was its president in 1997 and 1998), was a member of SAVE-A-TURTLE, and lives with many rescued cats and dogs. She's trained by the National Wildlife Rehabilitation Association and the International Wildlife Rehabilitation Council and is an instructor for the International Wildlife Rehabilitation Council. She has helped at oil spills, moved turtles' nests, and rescued countless birds and animals from all kinds of terrible circumstances, day and night. She and her cadre of dedicated, trained volunteers often helped in rescuing stranded dolphins or whales. The Wildlife Rescue's work is never done.

The new refuge also serves as an Environmental Education Center, hosting interns and groups of college students doing volunteer work on spring breaks.

In July 1998 Barron left the organization to do related rescue work in the Pacific Northwest, and the agency has since been "taken under the wing" of Suncoast Seabird Sanctuary in Indian Shores, the largest wild-bird hospital in the country. According to WRFK's new director, Debbie Brittin, a volunteer for four years, the Indian Shores–based sanctuary is helping financially and with supplies. Since August 1998, WRFK has been a subsidiary of the larger organization and will acquire a new building, which should be in place by the time of this book's publication. Shaped like a modular school building, this will be a climate-controlled hospital with office space and storage and food-preparation facilities. "This will keep the birds cooler; eventually we'll also get new equipment, including x-ray equipment," Brittin explains. WRFK has lost a valuable friend, but has gained improved facilities for its avian residents.

If you find an injured bird or small creature while you are in the Key West area, give this organization a call. Someone will respond quickly. Also, consider volunteering your time, money, or items constantly in demand like old towels and sheets, birdseed, dry cat food, and medical supplies.

Here are a few tips regarding what to do if you find an injured animal or bird:

- If you find a bird, be careful. Beaks and feet can be dangerous. Catch it with a net or a towel, cover its head, and deliver it to or call WRFK for pickup. If you snag a bird with a fishing line or a hook, do not release the bird until the line and hook are completely detached from the creature.

- Try not to handle injured birds or creatures, or handle them extremely gently. Keep them warm and quiet.
- If you find a sea turtle in danger, call the Florida Marine Patrol or WRFK for instructions. As these are rare or endangered, record the exact location and time, particularly if you must leave the animal. Keep the turtle cool by splashing water on the exposed areas.
- If you find a marine mammal like a whale or dolphin, do not return it to the ocean. Call the Florida Marine Patrol or WRFK. Keep the creature cool and wet by splashing water on its skin. Avoid blocking its blowhole, which is its airway.

The Wildlife Rescue is located in McCoy Indigenous Park, Key West, across from the White Street Pier. Take White Street to the pier, which stretches out into the ocean. On the left side of the street at the bottom, you'll see a parking lot and a sign for the park. Go through a wooden enclosed area that houses an office and rest rooms; the wildlife agency is out back to the right. Its hours are 9:30 A.M. to 4:00 P.M., seven days a week.

*For more information:* Call 305-294-1441.

# The Dry Tortugas National Park

The Dry Tortugas (*tortuga* means sea turtle) are a group of seven islands, 70 nautical miles west off Key West, the most prominent being 16-acre Garden Key. Las Tortugas were discovered in 1513 by Ponce de Leon. The word *dry* was added to warn seafarers that the islands contain no fresh water. They are part of a larger grouping, the Sand Keys. This latter group also includes the "near islands" just west of Key West and the

Marquesas, a ring of seven islands about 15 miles west of Key West. The area is accessible only by boat or seaplane.

You can make a day trip out here, or a half day, or you can camp in your tent for a week. If you love bird-watching, snorkeling, scuba diving, lounging on an almost empty sandy beach, or reading a novel a day, this may be just the place for you. On Garden Key are no restaurants, no inns, no Laundromats, no cars, no noise. No fresh water is available. This is primitive camping; grills, picnic tables, rest rooms, and a bookstore open a few hours a day are all the modern conveniences. Otherwise, you're on your own. It's the untouched Florida that you may have romanticized about but have not found elsewhere.

In 1832, John James Audubon visited the Dry Tortugas for the first time. This area was designated as a bird sanctuary in 1908. In 1992, President George Bush signed legislation to establish Dry Tortugas National Park.

The man-made highlight on Garden Key is Fort Jefferson, planned by Thomas Jefferson, built in the mid-1800s. It is America's largest coastal fort and is also the largest masonry structure in the Americas, sometimes called the "Gibraltar of the Gulf." This fortress is located on Garden Key, which is where the ferry or the seaplane lands. To build the fortress, workers transported 16 million bricks to this island, without benefit of sophisticated tools or equipment. There's a lighthouse, and inside the fort you'll see Dr. Samuel Mudd's dark prison cell. In case his name is not familiar, he treated John Wilkes Booth's broken leg and thus was considered a coconspirator in Abraham Lincoln's assassination. Imprisoned at the isolated fort on July 24, 1865, Mudd was pardoned by President Andrew Johnson in 1869.

The fort covers approximately 11 acres of Garden Key's 16 acres. Its outer wall is over a half mile long; its walls are more than eight feet thick. Three gun tiers were designed for 450 guns, but a shot was never fired from this fortification.

The bird life here is spectacular. More than 300,000 birds nest here each spring. Adjacent Bush Key is the only nesting ground for sooty terns and noddy terns in the contiguous United States. Between March and September every year, some 100,000 sooty terns gather on this key. Bush Key is closed to human visitors between March and October to allow these to birds to nest undisturbed. Other birds here include the brown pelican, which nests on Bush Key, the frigate bird on Long Key, and the masked booby on Hospital Key. You may see cattle egrets, a white egret about the size of a crow. In the spring on Garden Key tree, bank, or barn swallows may be seen air diving inside the fort.

This is also a nesting habitat for the endangered green, hawksbill, leatherback, and loggerhead sea turtles. Finally, more than 400 species of fish have been documented.

If you visit even more isolated Loggerhead Key, you may see lots of sea turtles. The largest island in the Tortugas, Loggerhead's plants and animals are all protected. The Loggerhead Lighthouse was built in 1858, and the waters off this island are particularly good for swimming, snorkeling, and diving.

Fewer than 50 species of land plants are found here because of salty soil, drought, and frequent storms. But that doesn't mean you won't see lovely vegetation. The trees include coconut and date palms, ancient buttonwood trees, gumbo limbo, a tiny relative of the poinsettia, prickly pear cactus, and night-blooming cereus (a cactus with a pungent blossom). The vegetation type is called beach-dune. Its natural state contains plants like sea oats, sea lavender, and other small bushes.

But the import of non-native plants such as the Australian pine has caused change; these tall trees shaded out much of the sun-loving native plants. The spreading roots of these big trees caused problems for the sea turtles that dig nests around the island. Today, the National Park Service is attempting to transform the island to its original natural state, removing some of these pines (also called casuarinas) but keeping some as roosting spots for hawks and other birds.

Although no one really lives at the Dry Tortugas National Park, park employees do stay here at least two years. If you have questions about plants or birds, they can surely help answer them.

The islands have two important seasons, a bit more dramatic than those of the more civilized Keys: winter storm season from December to March, and tropical storm season from June to November. April and May are nearly perfect.

To get to the Dry Tortugas, or more specifically Garden Key, you have primarily commercial options from Key West. You can board a 100-foot, high-speed ferry, which takes almost an entire day. On the ferry you will hear narration by a naturalist. Rates for the day trip on the *Yankee Freedom* include snorkel gear, round-trip transportation, breakfast, and lunch. Group and charter rates are available. This ferry also travels to Loggerhead Key one day a week and has a weekly dive day.

Or you can go the way we did—quickly, by seaplane. What a flight. Of course, this is not the most inexpensive option (about $160.00 per person for a half day), but I'd highly recommend it to anyone who has never flown in such a tiny vehicle. One of the companies which flies you there, Key West Air Service, has safe and beautiful six-passenger DeHavilland Beavers, which its pilots fly in Alaska during the summer months. The air trip takes under an hour and you fly approximately 500 feet above the ocean. During it, you wear a two-way headset, and the pilot speaks to you, pointing out sharks such as hammerheads, like slightly visible underwater ships below. As we spotted wild dolphins jumping, our friendly pilot said, "We're going to have a good day; dolphins mean good luck." One particularly nice touch is that the company gives each passenger a cooler with several soft drinks. The company will also loan snorkeling gear if you so desire. Your first view of the immense fort from the air is breathtaking.

To fly to the Dry Tortugas, call Key West Air Service at 305-292-5201. The toll-free number is 888-FLY-FORT. It offers several flights per day. You take the seaplane from its strip at 563 West College Road. To get there turn onto Route 1 north from Roosevelt Boulevard, then turn left at the first traffic light onto West College Road. Proceed approximately one-quarter mile and turn left into Sunset Marina.

If you choose to take the ferry, call 305-294-7009 or 800-634-0939. Boarding begins at 7:30 A.M.; departure time is 8:00 A.M. The ferry leaves from Land's End Marina at the foot of Margaret Street in Key West, just to the right of Mallory Dock. The ferry returns by 7:00 P.M.

Reservations are necessary for both trips. Last-minute cancellations are sometimes made due to weather or insufficient number of passengers.

The third option is to travel to the Dry Tortugas by private boat. If you wish to do so, you must bring all your fuel, water, and supplies. U.S. Coast Guard and Geodetic Survey Chart #11438 are necessary for navigation in the islands. There are no boat moorings or slips, and be sure to have a regular and a storm anchor.

Finally, look in the yellow pages for charter sailboat or other boat operators. All operators are licensed by the National Park Service to travel to this remote site.

*For more information:* Website: http://www.us-national-parks .net/dryt/dryt.htm.

# Key West National Wildlife Refuge

Key West National Wildlife Refuge, accessible only by boat, is located off the western shores of Key West. It includes the islands of the Lakes and the Marquesas. This was the first refuge established in the Florida Keys; it was designated as a preserve and breeding ground for native birds and wildlife in 1908. It now consists of more than 2,000 acres above high tide, 18,811 acres total. In 1975, all the islands of this refuge became a part of the National Wilderness Preservation System.

The Key West National Wildlife Refuge is one of four managed by the National Key Deer Refuge administrative office on Big Pine Key, which is part of the U.S. Department of the Interior's Fish and Wildlife Service.

This large refuge was established by an executive order signed by Theodore Roosevelt; it was created to preserve the habitat of colonial nesting birds, many of whom were killed for their feathers, used to adorn women's hats in the early 1900s. The great white heron almost became extinct because of this fashion trend.

The refuge consists of the Marquesas atoll (a ringlike island and reef that almost, or entirely, encloses a lagoon) and 13 other keys or islands; many are extremely isolated and inaccessible. Habitats include mangrove wetlands, berm hammocks, low hardwood hammocks, and salt marshes. Red mangrove roots surround these small keys, so all but the Marquesas, Boca Grande, and Woman Keys are virtually unreachable. You can walk a bit on the latter islands. These three have extensive beaches but have lured too many beachcombers and illegal campers in recent years, so the nesting and feeding areas of birds have become even more fragile. With the exception of portions of a couple of islands, the beaches are open to public access for wildlife-dependent activities, including wildlife observation and noncommercial photography. Areas closed to the public are clearly marked.

Terns, frigate birds, the endangered white-crowned pigeon, ospreys, and great white herons are protected at this refuge. Various raptors and the red-breasted merganser can also be found here. The sandy beaches are nesting habitat for the endangered Atlantic green and loggerhead sea turtles, and the indigenous mangrove diamondback terrapin, a three- to four-inch turtle, uses this refuge. These tiny carnivorous turtles only live below the Seven-Mile Bridge. Terrapins were, at the turn of the century, a well-known eating turtle, and their numbers are probably still only in the hundreds.

It's no wonder that people wish to take a boat out to visit these lush islands. The Marquesas atoll is called "the gem of the Florida Keys." It is one of the only two places in this country where yellowheart grows in the wild. This is a plant that may grow to a height of 35 feet with eight-inch-long compound leaves of five to seven leaflets. They have small male and female flowers with five greenish-white petals that bloom in June and July. Each leaflet has translucent glands.

Private vessels, kayaks, sailboats, or canoes do not require a special permit to enter backcountry waters; commercial ventures do. Off limits are airboats, hovercraft, floatplane landing, waterskiing, and "personal" boats, defined as shallow-draft, jet-drive watercraft operated by standing, sitting, or kneeling on or behind the vessel—in contrast to an operator standing or sitting inside a conventional boat.

Prohibited in all these refuges are commercial activity without a permit from the refuge manager, camping, firearms, metal detectors, removing artifacts, and abandoning and storing property. Of course, don't touch or remove any wildlife, either.

The best time to visit these keys is in the spring, fall, and winter months. Summer is much less enjoyable; mosquitoes and "no-see-ums" are extremely active throughout the lower Keys during this time.

*For more information:* To obtain maps, information, and regulations on how to get out to the refuge, contact the National Key Deer Refuge administrative offices in Big Pine Key at 305-872-2239. In addition, signs are posted at several boat ramps in the area.

# 5

# Nature Organizations

## Caribbean Conservation Corporation

The Caribbean Conservation Corporation (ccc) is a nonprofit organization dedicated to conserving sea turtles and other wildlife through research, education, advocacy, training, and preservation of natural areas. Although not actually located in the Keys, it often works with SAVE-A-TURTLE and the Turtle Hospital on common issues.

The ccc was founded in 1959 to support the research of internationally renowned naturalist and sea turtle biologist, the late Dr. Archie Carr, a zoology professor at the University of Florida who wrote 11 related books. Since that time, the organization has initiated and financed 25 projects in 16 countries, 5 regional projects, and many smaller programs and research studies. One such study tracks, by satellite, green turtles that nest in Florida, and another focuses on the impact of tourism on turtle-nesting beaches.

Aside from its administrative headquarters in Gainesville, the ccc has a 20,000-hectare preserve in Tortuguero National Park, Costa Rica. Its Sea Turtle Survival League engages in education, research, and advocacy on behalf of the nesting beaches of the Archie Carr National Wildlife Refuge, located between Melbourne and Wabasso, Florida.

*For more information:* Caribbean Conservation Corporation, 4424 N.W. 13th Street, Suite A-1, Gainesville, FL 32609. Call 352-373-6441 or 800-678-7853.

# Key Deer Protection Alliance (KDPA)

KDPA, a nonprofit organization, was formed in 1989 to help protect the endangered Florida Key deer. Its founders hoped to (1) provide accurate information about Key deer, (2) sponsor direct-action projects, and (3) preserve the deer's habitat. Current membership is about 300 from around the world. The organization is volunteer and tax exempt.

Some of the projects the KDPA has engaged in since its inception are the production of a wonderful 20-minute video, *The Key Deer Story*, available for $20.00; the award of scholarships to high school and college students interested in pursuing biological sciences; and the development of a slide presentation about the deer, which, with the video and a curriculum guide, KDPA placed in each public school media center and public library in Monroe County. Its members often make presentations to civil, social, or business organizations.

Its quarterly newsletter, *Alliance News*, provides articles about its activities and discusses relevant wildlife issues. In a recent issue was its mission statement: "The Alliance regards the Key deer as a national natural treasure to be protected as a legacy for future generations."

The organization has received many awards and grants since its inception, including one from the Nature Conservancy, a Special Achievement Award from the U.S. Fish and Wildlife Service, and a World Wildlife Fund Successful Communities Innovation Grant. A recent project, for which it received a matching grant from U.S. Fish and Wildlife, was building a wheelchair-accessible nature trail and raised viewing deck in the Key deer habitat in memory of Fred C. Mannillo, a long-time KDPA activist who used a wheelchair and who died in 1996. This trail, built by volunteers, was dedicated on August 22, 1997, on the 40th anniversary of the refuge.

*Key Deer*

*For more information:* P.O. Box 430224, Big Pine Key, FL 33043-0224.

## Lower Keys Friends of Animals

Lower Keys Friends of Animals helps domestic animals who are in trouble or pain in the lower Keys. But some of these animals have become wild because of dumping or overbreeding. Many cats live in mangroves, kept alive with daily feedings by Friends of Animals' volunteers.

The purpose of this nonprofit, all-volunteer organization is to offer free or low-cost spaying and neutering, help find lost animals, educate the public on pet responsibility, perform shelter intervention to ensure that animals are being properly cared for, urge dog licensing and enforcement of leash and abandonment laws, give financial assistance in some animal emergencies, and help find temporary or permanent homes for stray and unwanted animals. A new project provides free spaying and neutering for homeless people's dogs and cats.

Since I've been spending time in Key West, this agency has done amazing work, especially for the city's cats. When I first arrived, dozens of feral and homeless cats roamed the streets, each looking more emaciated and skittish than the next. It was not an uncommon sight to see a mother dumpster-diving for stale pizza to feed her kittens, which were huddling by the side of the road. Now many of these felines are humanely trapped, spayed, and released or provided with homes. You can tell if a cat has been neutered or spayed, because it has a tiny notch on its ear.

If you would like to help these creatures, look for food donation boxes at supermarkets like Fausto's Food Palace and cash donation boxes at stores like Cat House, Waterfront

Market, and City Zoo, all in Key West. Friends of Animals also holds an annual yard sale, generally in January. *For more information:* Call 305-292-5070.

# National Audubon Society, Tavernier Science Center

The National Audubon Society, a nonprofit organization dedicated to the study and protection of birds and to advocacy work, has a research facility in the upper Keys, in Tavernier. Of special concern to the staff of biologists are endangered and threatened species and bird-habitat loss, especially the loss of hammocks. Although the organization does not conduct bird walks, it is considering starting centers for ornithological education. The national organization has more than 500 chapters; in Florida there are several offices and a sanctuary called the Kissimmee Prairie Sanctuary, north of Lake Okeechobee.

Research biologist Rick Sawicki, who recently left the organization, conducted an eight-year study of the endangered white-crowned pigeon. This study has led the organization to a tropical flyways proposal, which would provide "stepping-stones for these birds, ... areas for them to be safe [and] eat" as they migrate within the Keys. The proposal envisions a network of hammock forest preserves in north Key Largo and the lower Keys that would provide feeding habitats during long flights, and refuge and cover for birds and for animal species that need these tracts for their survival.

The organization also sponsors an annual birdathon to count the species in the Keys. In April 1998, starting each morning around 3:00 A.M., Sawicki and a raft of volunteers, counted 118 types of birds. Visual or aural identifications included barn owl, pied-billed grebe, king rail, gray catbird, chuck-will's-widow, brown thrasher, red-breasted merganser, and La Sagra's flycatcher (extremely rare). The money raised through pledges or donations will enable Audubon to continue "to protect the last wild places in the Keys, the Everglades, and elsewhere."

The society has produced an excellent guide to good birding spots in the Keys, called "Birding in the Florida Keys," which you can pick up at its offices.

The center is located on Indian Mound Trail, on the bay side off Route 1 at MM 89, or power pole 550.

*For more information:* Tavernier Science Center, 115 Indian Mound Trail, Tavernier, FL 33070. Call 305-852-5092.

# Nature Conservancy of the Florida Keys

Since 1987, the Nature Conservancy (NC) has had a regional office in Key West and has already done lots of important work to protect and save the environment. The nonprofit organization's mission is "to preserve land and marine environments." It is a local resource for helping people become stewards or protectors of increasingly fragile natural resources. The NC has worked to clean up canals, to consider and negotiate the often opposing economic and environmental needs of the community, to encourage dive shops and fishers to help protect the reefs and Florida Bay, to work with scientists to monitor water quality, and to preserve—often by purchasing—remaining natural areas.

Although its office in Key West is relatively new, the Nature Conservancy has been a presence in the area since 1971 when it preserved Lignumvitae Key for public use. In recent history, it has assisted state programs in the purchase of hundreds of natural acres in the Keys, including land in the North Key Largo Hammocks, several tropical flyways, and several sites for Key deer protection on Big Pine Key.

A few recent activities include an on-the-water middle school education project in Florida Bay, a Florida Keys Invasive Exotics Task Force that is involved in setting priorities in state funding for removal of exotic plants, production of several publications on topics like coral reefs and the changing marine ecosystem, coordinated efforts with the U.S. Fish and Wildlife Service on behalf of the endangered Key deer, and much more.

The organization welcomes donations, supplies, and volunteers. Its office is located in a clapboard house on Front Street just south of the post office. The staff is responsive and knowledgeable; lots of complimentary literature is available about local and national environmental issues.

*For more information:* Nature Conservancy of the Florida Keys, 333 Fleming Street, Key West, FL 33040. The mailing address is P.O. Box 4958, Key West, FL 33041. Call 305-296-3880.

# Reef Environmental Education Foundation

Founded in 1990, Reef Environmental Education Foundation (REEF) is a nonprofit coral reef preservation organization of volunteer divers and snorkelers. The objective of this group is to train and use volunteers to collect information on reef fish biodiversity and distributions. Currently, the group has more than 8,000 members countrywide. The data it collects is housed at the University of Miami, which to date has more

than 12,000 hours of information on more than 300 species of
fish from its volunteer surveys. This data is available to government organizations, marine park managers, and other environmental organizations.

On Earth Day 1997 at an awards ceremony in the Keys,
REEF received an Environmental Hero Award for its services
from NOAA, the National Oceanic and Atmospheric Administration, and a letter of congratulations from Vice President
Al Gore.

Its goals for 1998 include continuing current projects,
increasing the number of seminars, and supporting activities
of this year's International Year of the Oceans campaign.
Fields surveys in 1998 included the Turks and Calicos Island,
the British Virgin Islands, Bonaire and Netherlands Antilles,
Grand Cayman, Texas Flower Gardens, St. Croix, Saba, and
two in the Keys, one from Key Largo to Key West and one
from Key West to the Dry Tortugas.

You can join this organization without paying a fee. As a
survey member, you receive an information packet, membership card, volunteer number, subscription to the *REEFNotes*
newsletter, and a personal access code to REEF's website.

If you wish to be a contributing member, you can do so for
$25.00 and up. These members may participate in a one-week
REEF field survey at a dive destination. The six-day field surveys in 1997, for example, included Marathon, Key Largo,
Islamorada, Dry Tortugas, Key West, and others farther afield.
In 1997 REEF monitored two new areas: Little Cayman and
Andros. Before your dive, you receive fish survey instructions
and a survey form, which includes more than 200 species of
fish. The form also includes questions about date, location,
temperature, visibility, and more. You are asked to explain the
habitat of your dive—open water, grass, rubble, etc. Survey-
ors receive an underwater slate and are asked to list only those

species they are most certain about. Experienced divers sometimes compile lists of more than a hundred species.

In 1996 a Key Largo Field Survey of 12 sites produced 163 species, including a pair of huge blue marlin and several large groupers. A 1996 Key West study yielded 167 species, including a rare jewfish and leopard gobies, only seen in the Key West area.

The operation's headquarters and visitor center are located in Key Largo, at MM 106 bay side, next to Diver's Outlet. *For more information:* REEF, P.O. Box 246, Key Largo, FL 33037. Call 305-451-0312. Website: http:www.reef.org.

# Reef Relief

Reef Relief, a nonprofit conservation membership organization, was founded in 1986 by skipper Craig Quirolo, current director of its marine projects, and celebrated its 10th anniversary in conjunction with "International Year of the Reef" in 1997. The organization is dedicated to preserving and protecting the Keys' Living Coral Reef. Reef Relief is perhaps most famous for its Mooring Buoy Program. One hundred sixteen reef mooring buoys at seven Key West area reefs have been installed and are regularly inspected and maintained by RR staff. This represents the largest privately maintained reef mooring program in the world.

The agency also is running a program, Photomonitoring Survey, being conducted by Craig Quirolo. This involves documenting changes in the endangered coral communities with a nonintrusive photographic and video survey. Quirolo discovered new coral diseases in this way, last year finding white plague type II, a quick-killing new threat. Next, he found white pox, which decimates elkhorn coral and spreads rapidly.

Scientists are now studying these diseases and the water quality in response to his important findings.

Like most of these conservation groups, an important aspect of Reef Relief's work is its educational mission. It offers several projects that teach about the importance—and the fragility—of the coral reef ecosystem, including mangrove forests, sea-grass beds, and the reefs themselves. It presents school programs as well as public programs.

Membership in Reef Relief includes newsletters, a bumper sticker, decal, action alerts, and other privileges. All contributions are tax deductible.

When you're in Key West, stop by the offices and shop at 201 William Street, next to the Waterfront Market on the gulf side of town. The shop is full of excellent posters, maps, T-shirts, books, and magazines related to the reef, and the friendly and well-informed staff are always willing to speak with you about how to help protect the Keys' fragile reef.

*For more information:* Reef Relief Environmental Center & Store, 201 William Street, P.O. Box 430, Key West, FL 33041. Call 305-294-3100. Website: www.reefrelief.org.

# Center for Aquatic Heritage

If you can't actually get into the waters surrounding Key West, and want to know what's going on down there, here's a way you can explore without even getting wet. Center for Aquatic Heritage is an informative and creative scuba website about life in the waters around Key West. Founded by a group of Key West scuba enthusiasts, this is their way of sharing information about their favorite part of the world. To date, the center has successfully launched several operations that have been broadcast on the Internet. The infrastructure includes a 63-foot dive vessel equipped with a computer and video production studio, underwater still and video cameras equipped with umbilical lighting systems, and other equipment needed to work at depths of more than 200 feet. Among the personnel are technical deep divers, photographers, paramedics, U.S. Coast Guard captains, and more. The center's long-term goal is to establish a mission that travels the oceans of the world, not only the waters surrounding Key West. But, as with most non-profit organizations, it always needs funding, supplies, and volunteers to continue.

The first goal is to educate young people by producing media they can tune in to learn about the welfare of the oceans. The ideal target age is between 7 and 13. The center will engage in "live-distance learning," video documentaries, television shows, and websites that teach environmental concepts and protection.

One example of its activities is sponsorship of an expedition to document and study the newly discovered sleeping sharks of the Keys. Scientists have long known that large, pelagic (open water) sharks sleep only where there is an unusually high oxygen content and at extreme depths. The discovery of such an area near Key West provides an opportunity for scientists to study these creatures. Starting in February 1997, scientists and divers began studying their habitat and dynamics around the clock for five days. This is the only known habitat where this behavior has been observed. Continuous observation was made possible through the use of Hibbard Marine ROVs (remote operated vehicles) at a site 10 miles offshore. Then, by Internet through Scuba World Online (www.scubaworld.com) and Key West Paradise (www.keywest.com), scientists and web watchers joined in this virtual expedition. William Trantham, coordinator of Marine Biology Technology Program at Florida Keys Community College, and college interns collected and archived the scientific data. Divers from Paradise Scuba also were on the team. The operational base was the live-aboard dive vessel *Tiburon* of Key West.

**For more information:** P.O. Box 6255, Key West, FL 33041. Call 305-293-9799. Website: http/www.scubaworld.com/cah/.

# Florida Keys National Marine Sanctuary

At 2,800 square miles (actually 3,674 square miles are partially protected), the Florida Keys National Marine Sanctuary is the largest in the country. Part of the National Marine Sanctuary Programs, its mission is to protect natural and cultural resources in marine environments. The larger mission of the program is "to identify, designate and manage areas of the marine environment of special national significance due to their conservation, recreational, ecological, historical, research, educational, or aesthetic qualities." Twelve such sanctuaries exist in the United States; two more are in development.

The Florida-based sanctuary stretches from the Everglades to Key West. The protected area is not marked, except on maps, and includes most of the diving spots noted in the Introduction. Although you might think the sanctuary would primarily protect coral reefs, it also includes fringing mangroves, sea-grass meadows, hard-bottom regions, path reefs, and bank reefs. A few species that live within the boundaries of the sanctuary are brain and star coral, grouper, turtle grass, spiny lobster, and loggerhead sponges.

The site was designated a national sanctuary in November 1990, and a series of strict regulations have been in effect since July 1, 1997. These regulations apply throughout the entire area of the sanctuary, including other protected areas and related zones. They focus on habitat protection, minimizing human impact on delicate species, and reducing threats to the water quality. The guardians of the sanctuary want to protect the areas from both direct and indirect threats—oil drilling, pollution, and more. The Sanctuary Advisory Council, which put together the regulations, consists of 22 members, including divers, commercial fishers, sportfishers, boaters, scientists, and the public.

Most of the area is still open to swimming, diving, and snorkeling; more than 90 percent of the sanctuary is open to fishing. Jet skis have been banned in the backcountry and will continue to be restricted in valuable habitat areas. A few sanctuary-wide prohibited activities include: removing, injuring, or possessing coral or life rock; diving or snorkeling without a dive flag; taking or possessing protected wildlife; and many more. No littering, please.

Four areas within the sanctuary are designated as only available for research projects: Conch Reef, Tennessee Reef, Looe Key, and Eastern Sambos Reef. No one may enter these areas unless bearing a valid permit.

This is an important sanctuary. Monroe County is one of four "hot spots" in the country in numbers of endangered species. The coral reef and its community are extremely endangered and becoming more diseased. This national protection of a large marine area of the Keys should help the natural world recover and survive.

*For more information:* The Center for Marine Conservation, Florida Keys Program, 8075 Overseas Highway, Marathon, FL 33050. Call 305-743-5199.

*Note:* Not all environmental news is bad. In June 1998, President Bill Clinton signed an executive order extending until 2012 an offshore oil drilling ban, originally due to expire in 2002.

Twelve national marine sanctuaries are covered by the order, including this one.

# Reading Guide

## Author's Short List

The books listed below offer further study and reflection on southern Florida's natural wonders. A good overall website for specific information on the Keys is http://fla-keys.com/index.htm.

Carr, Archie. *A Naturalist in Florida—A Celebration of Eden.* New Haven: Yale University Press, 1994.

Davidson, Osha Gray. *The Enchanted Braid, Coming to Terms with Nature on the Coral Reef.* New York: John Wiley and Sons, 1998.

Douglas, Marjory Stoneman. *Nine Florida Stories by Marjory Stoneman Douglas.* Edited by Kevin M. McCarthy. Jacksonville, Fla.: University of North Florida Press, 1990.

Douglas, Marjory Stoneman. *The Everglades—River of Grass.* New York: Rinehart & Co., 1947.

Jewell, Susan D. *Exploring Wild South Florida. A Guide to Finding the Natural Areas and Wildlife of the Everglades and Florida Keys.* Sarasota, Fla.: Pineapple Press, Inc., 1993.

Lazell, James D., Jr. *Wildlife of the Florida Keys, A Natural History.* Washington, D.C.: Island Press, 1989.

Murphy, George, editor. *The Key West Reader: The Best of Key West's Writers 1830–1990*. Key West: Tortugas, Ltd., 1989.

Ripple, Jeff. *The Florida Keys, The Natural Wonders of an Island Paradise*. Photographs by Bill Keogh and Jeff Ripple. Stillwater, Minn.: Voyageur Press, 1995.

Williams, Joy. *The Florida Keys*. 8th ed. New York: Random House, 1997.

# Index

# About the Author

Deborah Straw discovered and fell in love with the natural wonders of the Florida Keys several years ago. As Somerset Maugham said, "Sometimes a man hits upon a place to which he mysteriously feels that he belongs." The author spends two to three months a year in the Keys and the rest of her time in Vermont. A contributing editor to *laJoie*, a journal that fosters the appreciation of all creatures, Straw has written numerous nature-related articles, including ones for *Florida Keys Magazine*, *Amicus Journal*, and *Inner Voice*, and book reviews for *Solares Hill* in Key West. An inveterate traveler, she has also published dozens of travel articles in such publications as *Yankee*, *TravelSmart*, *Coffee Journal*, and *The Montreal Gazette*. When she's not in the Keys, she lives with her husband, a dog, and two cats in Burlington, Vermont.